WRITING
EROTIC
FICTION

Books in the 'Writing' series

Other books for Writers

WRITING EROTIC FICTION

Derek Parker

A & C Black · London

First published 1995
A & C Black (Publishers) Ltd,
35 Bedford Row, London WCIR 4JH

© 1995 Derek Parker

ISBN 0-7136-4046-4

A CIP catalogue record for this book is available
from the British Library.

Typeset in 10/12pt Palatino
Design by Janet Watson

Printed in Great Britain by Biddles Ltd,
Guildford, Surrey

Contents

Acknowledgements

The author is particularly grateful to Virgin and Headline plc for letting him see the results of surveys they have done into the readership of their erotic books. He is also grateful to the following authors and publishers in respect of passages listed:

William Burroughs and Transworld Publishers, for an extract from *The Soft Machine*.

Jilly Cooper and Transworld Publishers, for an extract from *Polo*.

Joe Orton and Reed International, for an extract from *Joe Orton's Diaries*.

Terry Southern and Messrs Marion Boyars Publishers Limited, London and New York, for an extract from *Blue Movie*.

Penguin Books Ltd and the Anaïs Nin Trust for an extract from *Delta of Venus*.

1
Choosing erotic fiction

Relatively few novels are published in which love does not play some part, and while many of them would not bring a blush to anybody's cheek it is impossible to think of any in which the sexual instinct is not at least by inference present. The extent to which it is present varies wildly, of course, and so does the way in which it is manifested. Thackeray and Thomas Mann could only allude very obliquely to masturbation; in our own time Phillip Roth and Brian Aldiss have written whole novels on the subject. The serious novelist can now be as crude or as modest as he or she wishes. The change in public opinion, mirrored if not by a change in the law at least by a change in the way it is administered, means that for the first time in our history writers can choose to write novels of which the entire purpose is to arouse sexual feelings, can be as subtle or as blatant as they wish, but can be confident that in the 1990s they are unlikely to be pilloried or prosecuted.

Indeed, it is now possible to publish a novel which only a decade or so ago would inevitably have been prosecuted, but which now is praised as a fine and admirable work of art: Alan Hollinghurst's gay novels *The Swimming Pool Library* (1988) and *The Folding Star* (1993) are cases in point. There can be no question that Mr Hollinghurst wrote his book simply to arouse the sexual feelings of his readers: it seems undeniable that most readers will have found the books erotic, and they are good example of the 'serious' novel containing highly erotic scenes.

On the other hand there are now many novels – as many as half a dozen or more are published each month – of which the whole purpose is, in the famous phrase of Sir Alan Herbert, 'to make the reader as randy as possible as quickly as possible' – and it is about writing this kind of literature that in this book I will make some suggestions. The 'serious novelist' (and I use that silly phrase because I can think of no other) may be left very much to him- or herself: the problems of writing an erotic scene in a conventional novel are the same as those of writing any other scene – with the exception of the difficulty of language (which I go into elsewhere, and which is not, anyway, quite the same for such a writer as for one who rather than five pages of erotica must turn out two hundred!).

Free to read, free to write

There is still some public feeling against specifically erotic books, which are usually described as 'pornographic', using the term pejoratively; a few people would want the word 'literature' to be placed in inverted commas whenever one is speaking of erotic books – which they seem to believe can never merit that description. I don't propose to spend a lot of time defending overtly erotic literature or those who choose to write it. People have always been free to read pornographic books; people should be free to write and publish them – and just as no-one is forced to read them, so no-one is forced to write them. Those who choose to do so will have their own motives, and they will be as various as the motives which persuade us to write other kinds of books – to make money, because we think they will sell, because we enjoy writing them, because we *can* write them. The motives of the readers are simple: they buy and read erotica because they enjoy it – they like being sexually aroused, whether in order to enjoy sex more with their partners or because they enjoy masturbating and find that these books add to that pleasure.

Erotic or pornographic novels (and we will return to these definitions later) are now unlikely to be prosecuted, though the law under which they can be indicted is still in force. This is a relatively recent development: some Members of Parliament and the judiciary, and some members of the public, would still wish to prosecute writers and publishers of erotica. But those 'ordinary people' sworn in as jurors in the most recent cases brought against authors and publishers have simply declined to find for the prosecution, and the law has (at the time of writing) fallen into almost complete disuse.

The law against published books which tend to 'deprave and corrupt' readers was well exercised in the early years of this century, and authors and booksellers regularly fell foul of it. Perhaps the most notorious case of the prosecution of an entirely serious and inoffensive novel was that, in 1928, of Radclyffe Hall's *The Well of Loneliness*, an account of a lesbian love affair which was almost ostentatiously reticent (the only suggestive line in it, about the two women lovers, was 'And that night they were not divided'). The Chief Magistrate at Bow Street, Sir Chartres Biron, referred twenty times, in his judgement, to 'horrible', 'vile', 'filthy' and 'unnatural' practices, and ordered the confiscation of all copies of the book. It was two decades before it could be republished.

Many little comedies were played out during those twenty years – local magistrates in English towns ordered the confiscating and burning of books by Rabelais and Flaubert, Maupassant and Defoe, Angela Thirkell and Erskine Caldwell. In 1953, Secker and Warburg were prosecuted (at the behest of the then Director of Public Prosecutions, Sir Toby Matthew) for publishing Stanley Kauffman's *The Philanderer*, a highly moral novel in which the most obscene phrase described a woman's 'lovely lemon-shaped breasts'. Happily, the case was heard by the sensible Mr Justice Stable, who in his summing-up came down on the side of the publishers, who were found not guilty. The book's sales rocketed.

Not all judges were as liberal in their views as Mr Justice Stable, and in the following years there were several successful prosecutions, some of his fellow judges seizing the opportunity to fulminate against books that (as one of them put it) 'polluted the fountain of our national blood'.

Lady Chatterley's Lover

The most famous case, and the one which foreshadowed the end (at least for the time) of the persecution of publishers and authors, was of course that brought against Penguin Books in 1959 for publishing an unexpurgated edition of D. H. Lawrence's *Lady Chatterley's Lover*. The Obscene Publications Act allowed for the publication of books to be defended on the grounds that it was 'for the public good' – the good of literature, art or learning. No-one interested in the history of censorship should fail to read the account of the trial edited by C.H.Rolph and published by Penguin – one of the great comedies of our time.

The scandal seems to have been, in the minds of the prosecution, mainly that the book was to be made available for sale at three shillings and sixpence (under twenty pence), which meant that it was likely to fall into the hands of ordinary, uneducated readers who – unlike members of the Establishment – would certainly be damaged by it, not having the intellectual faculties to defend themselves against corruption. Unhappily for the prosecution, the jury consisted largely of just such people, and they brought in a resounding verdict of not guilty.

A few more prosecutions tottered into court in the 1960s, most notably that of Hubert Selby Jr's *Last Exit to Brooklyn*, a horrifying account of sexual degradation in the drug-infested streets of New York, particularly focusing on homosexual destitutes. The judiciary was worried about prosecution – mainly, it seems (as in the case of an earlier publication, of Henry Miller's *Tropic of Cancer*) because of the long list of distinguished people the defence planned to call as witnesses to the literary value of the book; the D.P.P. decided against a prosecution, and it was left to the Baptist lay preacher and property developer Sir Cyril Black M.P. to bring one privately.

The case was a highly entertaining one. The defence relied on witnesses such as Anthony Burgess and Frank Kermode; the prosecution on Sir Basil Blackwell, the Oxford bookseller – who claimed that, at 77, he had been depraved and corrupted by reading the book – and the then Captain Robert Maxwell M.P., who thought it 'muck and filth' (but revealed in cross-examination that he had never heard of *The Decameron*, which perhaps a little devalued his view on literary merit).

Leo Gradwell, the Marlborough Street magistrate, found for the prosecution and ordered the destruction of the book. However, the publisher, John Calder, was able to continue to publish it outside the jurisdiction of the Marlborough Street Court, and the Attorney-General felt he must now bring a prosecution. In December 1967 an Old Bailey jury also found against the book – but the decision was reversed by the court of appeal, and as a result of such publicity as money could not have bought, the book sold in its hundreds of thousands.

Enter President Nixon

In America, there were similar developments. Perhaps the most comic example concerned the Presidential Commission on Obscenity and Pornography which President Nixon set up in 1968, on which sat a number of members who might have been expected to be extremely antagonistic to erotic writing (a Methodist Minister, a rabbi, a Catholic priest known for publicly demonstrating against pornography, and the President of Morality in Media, Inc).

When the Commission reported, the President was horrified to discover that it recommended the American Government abolish all laws that sought to deprive adults of the right to see or read any and all so-called obscene materials. President Nixon immediately decided to reject the Commission's recommendations: 'So long as I am in the White House,' he said, 'there will be no relaxation of the national effort to control and eliminate smut from our national life. . . The Commission contends that the proliferation of filthy books and plays has no lasting, harmful threat on man's character. . . Centuries of civilisation and ten minutes of common sense tell us otherwise.'

However, an enterprising Californian publisher, William Hamling, had the brilliant idea of producing a glossy paperback illustrated edition of the Commission's Report, and J. Edgar Hoover, the Director of the F.B.I., a gentleman whose collection of obscene literature was considerable, and whose private predilection seems to have been for dressing up in women's clothing, promptly advised the President to prosecute Hamling for obscenity. Faced with having to decide that the Commission's report on obscenity was itself obscene, the jury found a way out by convicting Hamling for publishing a brochure advertising it, fined him $87,000 and sent him to prison for four years.

The end of prosecution?

Both in America and Britain, it has become clear during the past twenty years that the law has no stomach for a fight, either against books in which detailed descriptions of sex are part of a more conventional story, or those which are erotic or pornographic in the sense that their whole purpose is to arouse the reader. Cases such as the one brought against the Oz 'school kids' issue in 1970, and The Little Red Schoolbook a year later, were phlegmatically viewed by the general public as the final panting protests of those who still lived, anachronistically, in an age when sex was regarded as a sin rather than as a pleasure. The objections roused by such campaigners as Mrs Mary Whitehouse seemed to have (in the words of John Mortimer, the creator of Rumpole and the defending barrister in a number of anti-pornography cases) 'all the charm of a wander around an old house built in about 1850, when the definition of obscenity was first promulgated'.

Some writers have always chosen, or have been forced, to deal with sexuality obliquely – when Jane Austen speaks of 'happiness' in marriage it is clear that she means sexual happiness, but it would have been impossible for a novelist of her time, certainly a woman novelist, to have dealt with sex other than indirectly – even should she wish to do otherwise. Increasingly in modern times, some writers, women among them, have dealt with sexuality with a frankness that can even today be shocking at least to the older generation of readers.

The problems of writing a book attempting to advise authors on dealing with the erotic element in fiction, and on writing books in which the erotic elements are the main content, are not however mainly legal. In the first place, the fact that a description of love-making as a physical activity is only a part of most books presents its own difficulties: writing a book advising other writers how to deal with that appears to be like attempting to produce a treatise on 'how to write dinner party scenes'. There are however practical points to be made and suggestions to be offered. And perhaps in erotic writing more than in any other *genre* – but certainly as much – it is absolutely necessary for anyone thinking of attempting it to know as much as possible about the work others, of previous generations as well as the present one, have done. The extracts included here are not simply a means of filling space.

There are also moral questions, some of which must be addressed – and, as with violence, the question to what extent books containing graphic descriptions of sexual activity may or may not influence the reader (something, in the present day, too important to be neglected).

Political incorrectness

One final note, before we start: in a book about sexual behaviour and activity (even this kind of book) the danger of offending women is obviously omnipresent, and 'political correctness' (whatever that phrase now means) may be almost impossible to achieve. It is all too easy to understand why women have often been affronted by male pornography, for in it they have too frequently been regarded as 'sex objects' – mere aids to masturbation – though this is probably more true of visual than verbal pornography. I have no wish to praise this kind of writing, much less encourage it; but to disregard it would be stupid. It is however interesting and instructive that in erotic books written by women (including those recently written and published specifically to be read by women) not only have men been treated in the same way – and why not? – but there is no shortage of scenes in which women are similarly handled. Maybe what might in cold blood be regarded as 'degradation' is an essential part of sexual fantasy, whether male or female?

I need hardly say that since erotic literature is now being written by men and women, this book is directed at both sexes; I shall some-times say 'he' and sometimes 'she'. Any reader who feels that when alluding to one sex I am disregarding the other will be mistaken.

2
Why write erotic books?

What do we mean when we call a book erotic?

Let's look first at the extreme – the erotic novel whose purpose is, more or less simply, to *be* erotic. And before we go any further, we should define some terms. What is 'erotic' to one reader is 'pornographic' to another and 'obscene' to a third. Are these terms interchangeable?

Only up to a point. The publishers of this book requested me to look at various ways of writing erotic prose. They did not commission a book on how to write pornography. Other publishers have their lists of 'the best in erotic fiction', but I think would be unwilling to advertise themselves as pornographers. I cannot be alone in detecting a slightly mealy-mouthed approach to the subject: after all, the terms are not so far apart in meaning.

The word 'erotic' derives from the Greek *erotikos*, itself from *eros*, meaning, simply, 'sexual love'. However, various modern English dictionaries differ in defining it. *The Oxford English Dictionary* says 'of or pertaining to the passion of love; concerned with or treating of love; amatory.' *The Concise Oxford* adds 'esp. tending to arouse sexual desire or excitement.' *The Penguin English Dictionary* says 'of or concerned with sexual life', and adds 'amorous'. *Webster's* mentions 'literary or artistic items having an erotic theme, esp. books treating of sexual love in a sensuous or voluptuous manner.'

The word 'pornography' has a more complicated history. It seems to have derived from the Greek *porne*, meaning 'prostitute', and *graphos*, meaning 'writing' – this seems to hint at literature doing what a prostitute does: arousing and hopefully helping to satisfy one's sexual instincts and emotions. But it has also been pointed out that the derivation may more accurately be from *porno*i, a class of hooker rather below the prostitute, and therefore a term of abuse. However that may be, the connection with prostitution has been stressed by almost every modern dictionary: *Webster's*, for instance, says 'a depiction (in writing or painting) of licentiousness or lewdness: a portrayal of erotic behaviour designed to cause sexual excitement.' *The Oxford Reference Dictionary* is equally definite, and adds an interesting gloss: 'the explicit representation of sexual activity visually or descriptively to stimulate erotic *rather than aesthetic* feelings; pictures or literature containing this.' (The italics are mine).

The Latin *obscenus* seems to be the root of 'obscene'. The original meaning of *obscenus* is obscure; but today it is generally a term used to condemn anything which the speaker or writer finds morally objectionable: as *The Oxford Reference Dictionary* bluntly puts it, 'offensively indecent', or (*Penguin*) 'indecent, lewd; disgusting; referring too frankly or offensively to sex.'

An obscene libel

Since 1727 it has been, in English law, a crime to publish 'an *obscene* libel'. The first prosecution on these grounds, in 1708, was of a printer named Reid, for publishing a book entitled *The Fifteen Plagues of a Maidenhead*; but the Lord Chief Justice of the King's Bench, Sir John Holt, ruled that while he disliked the book, it was not illegal to publish it. Obscenity was a spiritual offence, and could be punished only by the ecclesiastical courts. (Holt seems, of course, now to be right: if obscenity is an offence, it seems proper to call it an offence against the spirit).

Nearly twenty years later, in 1725, the law had more success with *Venus in the Cloister, or the Nun in her Smock*, written by an unfrocked priest, François de Chavigny de la Bretonniére, and published by a certain Edward Curll (together with *A Treatise of the Use of Flogging in Venereal Affairs*). *Venus in the Cloister* 'revealed' the sexual orgies in which Catholic priests and nuns indulged under cover of Roman rites.

The prosecution seems to have been on political rather than moral grounds, but at all events the judge considered both books likely to 'weaken the bonds of civil society, virtue and morality'. Curll spent some time in the pillory at Charing Cross, whence many readers made their way to cheer him, offer him food and drink, and even sing to him. A description of the trial, which resulted in the establishment in 1857 of the Obscene Publications Act, can be found in Donald Thomas' *A Long Time Burning* (1969). In 1736 Chief Justice Cockburn defined 'obscene' in the following terms: 'I think the test of obscenity is this, whether the tendency of the matter charged as obscenity is to *deprave and corrupt* those whose minds are open to such immoral influences, and into whose hands a publication of this sort may fall' – the first appearance of the notorious phrase which I have italicised.

It was clear from the first that judges and barristers did not believe *their* minds open to corruption; they were out to protect less educated and therefore more susceptible minds. Though the terms of the law were later altered to protect 'those who may in all the circumstances read the book', Cockburn's attitude has survived well into our own time: we have only to remember the question put to the jury by the senior Treasury Counsel, Mr Mervyn Griffith-Jones, during the *Lady Chatterley* trial: 'Is it a book you would wish your wife or your servant to read?' 'Obscene' remains probably the most denigratory of words when applied to a book – and its power in the minds of the Establishment has led to some pretty farces.

Our own shorthand

But to return to the present, perhaps we need, for the purposes of this book, our own shorthand. I propose to use the word 'obscene' when I mean that a book or a passage is, even to the most open-minded reader, likely to be offensive not merely through a description of cruel or degrading acts, but because of the rankness and vulgarity of the language. By 'pornographic' I shall mean writing which is purely masturbatory in purpose – though there are really few distinctions to separate the erotic and the pornographic. All effective erotic writing may be (in the famous phrase) read with one hand, and the purpose of all erotic writing must be, more or less, to excite one's amorous propensities (as Dr Johnson remarked of the bosoms of actresses). Pornographic books may be coarse, humourless, crude, but some of the most elegant erotic prose is designed to serve the same purpose, and though the two terms seem to me to be almost interchangeable, I shall generally use 'pornographic' as a mildly denigratory term.

Most obscene and some pornographic literature seems to me likely, with good reason, to offend women (and indeed sensitive men). Erotic writing, in the sense in which I shall refer to it, is another matter. By 'erotic' I shall mean writing which may sometimes describe coarse or even bestial acts, and which will be designed to convey sexual emotions to the reader and arouse them in him or her; but which will celebrate the beauty of the human body and the pleasures of love-making, and be positive in doing so. Love, incidentally, is not a prerequisite of the erotic novel. As in life, sex in literature can be enjoyable and satisfying quite apart from love, though the fact that it is most satisfactory within a loving relationship is no less true because the moralists are always insisting upon the fact – or indeed because some pornographers share that view.

Pornography and women

This is as good a place as any to grasp once more, if briefly, the nettle of 'political correctness', and the offence given to many women by some erotic books. The various women's movements have quite properly been extremely active where both pictorial and literary pornography is concerned, and have in the main, with a few exceptions, condemned it. The question whether erotic writing must always and necessarily denigrate women is a silly one; the answer is so clearly in the negative. But it is equally clearly necessary to discuss how offence may be given and how one may avoid giving it.

The reason why male writers have so often, and women writers so rarely, depicted the opposite sex exclusively as a means of sexual gratification, is clearly associated with the traditional part men have played in society as the sexual aggressor; and also with the fact that surviving books (and indeed paintings) are so predominantly the work of men. There is plenty of evidence, nevertheless, to suggest that women's interest in erotica – both as writers and readers – is at least as keen as men's, though often it is of a different nature. So while it might be inaccurate to suggest that as many women will read this book with a view to actually using it as men, I do not intend to suggest that none will – indeed, a number of women writers have shown a very keen interest in portraying sexual activity as graphically as possible, and some with pornographic vigour.

Why erotica?

Very little writing is published unless there is a demand for it. Erotica is as old as literature itself: a highly erotic description of the love-making of the goddess Inanna and the shepherd Dumuzi is inscribed in cuneiform script on Sumerian clay tablets four thousand years old. Ancient Egyptian love poetry can still stir a modern reader. A century after the invention of movable type Pietro Aretino (1492-1557) published his *Sonnetti Lussuriosi* (incidentally, he is said to have died as a result of falling backward off his chair while listening to his sister's obscene stories).

Humankind has always used sex not only for procreation but for pleasure. We, or many of us, enjoy reading about travel or sport or food because good books on those subjects remind us of the pleasures of the cruise or the tennis court or the table, and even make those pleasures keener, suggesting the means of enjoying more and better holidays, games or meals in the future. We enjoy reading books on sexual activity for much the same reasons.

It is important too to remember the part erotic writing has played in the education of young men, in particular. John Cleland's delightful eighteenth century novel, *Fanny Hill, or the Memoirs of a Woman of Pleasure*, is said to have educated generations of young Americans in sexual behaviour at a time when it was impossible that sex should be mentioned in school, and when (as is still too often the case) it was as rarely mentioned at home. More recently such books as *The Joy of Sex* and even *The Happy Hooker*, both of which are certainly often read as a means of titillation, have been valuable in telling young (and indeed older) people about aspects of sexuality concerning which there is still too often a conspiracy of silence. Sex information is often given only in terms which children will fail to understand, and which will therefore not corrupt them.

Sex and characterisation

But there are other reasons for writing about sex than for titillation or education. Just as a description of a character's attitude to food or music or landscape may enrich and enlarge our knowledge and understanding of him or her, so it is with sexuality. This does not of course mean that a writer need necessarily go into detail about the sexual activities of a character. During periods when it was impossible to publish erotic material, good writers found ways of expressing the sexual drives and preferences of their characters without offending the censors: we know all we need to know about the sexual charisma of Vronsky and its effect on Anna Karenina without needing to learn what they did in bed. The highly charged sado-masochistic relationship between Bill Sikes and Nancy in *Oliver Twist* would not necessarily have been improved by graphic sexual description. But though it is doubtful whether Tolstoy felt the need to be more explicit, behind Dickens' Victorian sentimentality roared great banks of sexual energy which he might have expressed more overtly had that been possible. And no-one can read Emily Brontë without sensing that, though she would not necessarily have used specifically sexual terms, the sexual emotion boiling in *Wuthering Heights* was not comprehensively expressed in the language she was able to use.

However, for many novelists, inference is enough: when Emma, the eponymous heroine of Jane Austen's novel, reflects on Jane Fairfax's engagement to Frank Churchill, she says: 'She loves him then excessively, I suppose. . . Her affection must have overpowered her judgement.' The allusion to sexual attraction could hardly be clearer. Who knows whether Austen, living today, might not have welcomed the opportunity to be more explicit? In a recently discovered letter to her friend Martha Lloyd, written not long before her death in 1817, she gave a description of a man she had met in Bath, perhaps a hairdresser, with whom she had 'enjoyed the warmest of relations': 'He seemed to care for his own hair as much as the tresses of others – but his deftness of touch, and his movement – such strength, but gentle too – across the Pump [Room] is now forever with me. . .' Something more here than the usual, cool Austen touch.

Trollope manages to convey the emotions of his heros and heroines without being explicit, and makes his meaning perfectly clear. In *The Prime Minister*, Emily Wharton says to Arthur Fletcher, 'I have trembled when I have heard your voice. My heart has beat at the sound of your footsteps as if it would burst. . .' – and Arthur is in no doubt that that means: 'hot, passionate love.'

Some writers of earlier ages would certainly have welcomed the opportunity to be more open and frank about the sexuality of their characters. Edith Wharton, for example, could as we know write with the utmost passion about the sexual act (she did so in the fragments of a novel, *Beatrice Palmato*, unpublished and unpublishable until years after her death). She might have written with similar passion in *Summer*, her 1914 novel about the sexual awakening of a young Massachusetts girl, had it been possible. As it was, the most she could do was to speak of 'the melting of palm into palm and mouth to mouth, and the long flame burning from head to foot.' On the other hand one cannot imagine her friend Henry James writing a truly erotic passage (though it is worth seeking out Louis Wilkinson's brilliantly funny parody, *The Better End*, which convincingly suggests how such a passage might have turned out).

The greatest authors, from Dante onward, have felt the need to write about sex as intimately as possible. However, Dante, when he wrote in *The Divine Comedy* of Francesca's adultery, did so with great restraint, showing as many other writers have since done that one can deal with sexuality without the slightest possibility of giving offence even to the most sensitive reader. Homer did so too, almost three thousand years ago, in the *Iliad* (Book XIV), when he described the goddess Here attempting to seduce Zeus:

> 'She began by removing every stain from her comely body with
> ambrosia, and anointing herself with the delicious and imperishable
> olive oil she used. It was perfumed and had only to be stirred in the
> Palace of the Bronze Floor for its scent to spread through heaven and
> earth. With this she rubbed her lovely skin; she combed her hair, and

with her own hands plaited her shining locks and let them fall in their divine beauty from her immortal head. . .'

Unsurprisingly, Zeus succumbed, and

'the gracious earth sent up fresh grass beneath them, dewy lotus and crocuses, and a soft and crowded bed of hyacinths, to lift them off the ground. In this they lay, covered by a beautiful golden cloud, from which a rain of glistening dewdrops fell.'

'Books are well written, or badly written'

There is no rule which suggests that restraint in describing erotic emotions or situations necessarily results in 'good writing', and explicit descriptions in 'bad writing'. At his trial, Oscar Wilde put the matter in a nutshell. He was being questioned by the prosecution about a short erotic story entitled *The Priest and the Acolyte*, which had appeared in a magazine to which he had also contributed. The prosecuting counsel, Edward Carson, Q.C., asked whether he thought the story was immoral. Wilde replied 'It was worse; it was badly written'. He later remarked that 'In writing a play or a book, I am concerned entirely with literature – that is, with art. . .' When Carson quoted Wilde's aphorism 'There is no such thing as a moral or an immoral book. Books are well written, or badly written', and asked whether it was really the author's view that an immoral book, well written, could be a good book, the author replied 'Yes, if it were well written so as to produce a sense of beauty, which is the highest sense of which a human being can be capable. If it were badly written, it would produce a sense of disgust.' Anyone with a reasonable experience of considering erotic literature will nod the head in agreement, and will also agree that pornography can be ill or well written, just as travel writing may.

The long-lasting sanctions against the publication of erotic literature in the West drove much good erotic writing underground. Clandestine publishers, being more concerned with making money than publishing good literature, allowed more examples of ill written and illiterate rubbish to survive from the last century than of good writing – though after 1900, some good writing was published. Aubrey Beardsley's *Under the Hill* is an example; it was expurgated when it first appeared in the *Savoy*, but an unexpurgated edition came out as early as 1907. It contained some passages which struck a genuinely pagan erotic note – describing for instance Venus' amorous play with her pet unicorn, Adolphe:

'Poor Adolphe! How happy he was, touching the Queen's breasts with his quick tongue-tip. I have no doubt that the keenest scent of animals must make women much more attractive to them than to men; for the gorgeous odour that but faintly fills our nostrils must be revealed to the brute creation in divine fullness. Anyhow Adolphe sniffed as never a man did around the skirts of Venus. After the first charming interchange of affectionate delicacies was over, the unicorn lay down upon his side, and, closing his eyes, beat his stomach wildly with the mark of manhood

'Venus caught that stunning member in her hands and lay her cheek along it; but few touches were wanted to consummate the creature's pleasure. The Queen bared her left arm to the elbow, and with the soft underneath of it made amazing movements horizontally upon the tightly-strung instrument. Tannhauser was amused to learn that the etiquette of the Venusburg compelled everyone to await the outburst of these venereal sounds before they could set down to *déjeuner*.

'Adolphe had been quite profuse that morning.

'Venus knelt where it had fallen, and lapped her little aperitif!'

The use of the sense of smell in erotic literature is still sparing; this is a good example of it. How surprising, incidentally, to find such an ostentatious reference to semen, in such a context, in a book published and unprosecuted, almost ninety years ago.

In the novel *Teleny*, in which Oscar Wilde seems to have had a hand (if only perhaps as editor), the writer or writers have passages which while almost clinically descriptive are not without intensity. One of them brings to an end a scene in a horse-drawn cab, in which the narrator and his new acquaintance, Teleny, a concert pianist, masturbate each other. It is singular for a particular reason:

'. . .Our nerves were so strained, our excitement had reached such a pitch, and the seminal ducts were so full, that we felt them overflowing. There was, for a moment, an intense pain, somewhere about the root of the penis, or rather, within the very core and centre of the reins, after which the sap of life began to move slowly, slowly, from within the seminal glands; it mounted up the bulb of the urethra, and up the narrow column, somewhat like mercury within the tube of a thermometer – or rather, like the scalding and scathing lava within the crater of a volcano.

'It finally reached the apex; then the slit gaped, the tiny lips parted, and the pearly, creamy fluid oozed out – not all at once in a gushing jet, but at intervals, and in huge, burning tears.

'At every drop that escaped out of the body, a creepy almost unbearable feeling started from the tips of the fingers, from the ends of the toes, especially from the innermost cells of the brain; the marrow in the spine and within all the bones seemed to melt; and when the different currents – either coursing with the blood or running rapidly up the nervous fibres – met within the phallus (that small instrument made out of muscles and blood-vessels) a tremendous shock took place, a convulsion which annihilated both mind and matter, a quivering delight which everyone has felt, to a greater or lesser degree - often a thrill almost too intense to be pleasurable.'

The passage seems to have been written less to arouse the reader than to attempt to convey in some detail the physical and psychological emotions which accompany orgasm; and no-one could claim that it does not to some extent succeed. It is difficult to think of a parallel example as graphic or indeed as effective. The passage, which is distinctly arousing, ends on a strangely cool note and creates a plateau between that scene and another, even more overtly exciting scene.

There is no reason at all, then, why erotic prose should not be as well written as prose in any other métier; nor that well-written erotic books should not sell as well as scatological rubbish. And writers, realising the fact, have often been quite frank about it when that has been possible. Shakespeare's contemporary, Thomas Lodge, advertised his erotic poem *Scillaes Metamorphosis* as 'verie fit for young Courtiers to peruse, and coy Dames to remember'. Shakespeare's *Venus and Adonis*, wildly popular when it came out in 1593, was not only a conscious attempt to please Shakespeare's young patron Southampton (and what young man would not have been complimented to be likened to an Adonis hotly pursued by the goddess of love?) but an equally conscious effort to capture the custom of sophisticated readers eager for an amorous tale. And it *is* a splendidly amorous tale: had its equivalent been published in, say, the 1950s, what view would have been taken of such passages as that in which Venus compares her body to a park in which her lover is invited to graze?

'Feed where thou wilt, on mountains or in dale.
  Graze on my lips – and if those hills be dry
  Stray lower, where the pleasant fountains lie.

'Within this limit is relief enough -
Sweet bottom-grass and high delightful plain,
Round rising hillocks, brakes obscure and rough,
To shelter thee from tempest and from rain. . .'

Obscenity and quality

In our own time some writers who have been most 'frank' about sex have after initial outbursts of horror from the puritans been generally accepted as having literary quality. Their publications vary, and ironically by no means always fall firmly within my definition of the 'erotic', for their work has often been extremely scabrous. They are inventive and original in style, but where sex (a very prominent aspect of their writing) is concerned, they are notable more for the vigour with which they describe often sadistic or masochistic scenes than for any celebration of loving sensuality. Take, for instance, Henry Miller and William Burroughs, perhaps the two most celebrated erotic writers of the first half of this century. Miller (1891-1980) wrote *Tropic of Cancer* and *Tropic of Capricorn* in the 1930s, but they were banned in the US and Britain until the 1960s. Few people could deny that his work is obscene in the sense that it continually degrades women. Though he seems himself to have been a gentle man more confused about his own sexuality than delighting in it, in his writing he continually pokes fun at women, humiliates and demeans them:

> 'Moving with furious abandon, biting my lips, my throat, my ears, repeating like a crazed automaton, "Go on, give it to me, go on, give it, go on, oh God, give it, give it me!" she went from one orgasm to another, pushing, thrusting, raising herself, rolling her ass, lifting her legs and twining them round my neck, groaning, grunting, squealing like a pig, and then suddenly, thoroughly exhausted, begging me to finish her off, begging me to shoot. "Shoot it, shoot it. . . I'll go mad." Lying there like a sack of oats, panting, sweating, utterly helpless, utterly played out, that she was, I slowly and deliberately rammed my cock back and forth, and when I had enjoyed the chopped sirloin, the mashed potatoes, the gravy and all the spices, I shot a wad into the mouth of her womb that jolted her like an electric charge.[1]

I have already suggested a comparison between writing about sex and writing about food: that passage really makes the woman sound like an unconsidered meal greedily thrown down without thought, without tasting it. Good writing? – perhaps. In 1942 George Orwell suggested that Miller was 'the only imaginative prose-writer of the slightest value who has appeared among the English-speaking races for some years past.' But I would certainly propose that Miller is not a good *erotic* writer. Even the urgency is that of lust rather than sensuality. I find it difficult to believe that most readers would not find the passage I have quoted repulsive rather than arousing.

William Burroughs (1914 -) is an even stronger example of the (to a degree) seriously regarded author who it is difficult to admire as an erotic writer. His *The Naked Lunch*, *The Soft Machine* and other books are highly experimental in their use of 'cut-out' and 'fold-out' techniques, the use of dreams, and in general an attachment to the surreal; and certainly his accounts of heroin addiction (especially in an early book, *Junkie*) are vivid and effective. However, his

[1] Henry Miller, *Sexus* (1970)

descriptions of homosexual couplings (whether real or imaginary) are frequently more obscene than erotic – scenes of violence, hanging in particular (the fact that hanged men frequently reveal erections seems almost uniquely to have fascinated twentieth century homosexual writers) – and while often intense are perhaps too brutal to appeal to more than a minority of readers in the way of arousing sexual emotion. The experimental nature of the prose itself also lessens the impact of the eroticism, as far as the reader is concerned.

> 'So there we are in the train compartment shivering junk sick our eyes watering and burning and all of a sudden the sex chucks hit me in the crotch and I sagged against the wall and looked at Johnny too weak to say anything it wasn't necessary he was there too and without a word he dipped some soap in warm water and dropped my shorts and rubbed the soap on my ass and worked his cock up me with a corkscrew motion and we both came right away standing there and swaying with the train clickety clack clack spurt spurt into the brass cuspidor.'[2]

It is certainly possible to find such passages vivid and interesting displays of literary technique. Both Burroughs and Miller will certainly appeal to some readers as interesting writers, and to others whose sexual inclinations match their own. As erotic writers, however, their work will be caviar to the general. The situations and incidents described by Jean Genêt (1910-86) are often quite as 'nasty', but the 'unpleasantness' must be balanced against the elegance of his style and the beauty of his prose, which is often remarkable. For instance, writing of his youth in *The Thief's Journal*, he sees a workman of about his own age spit on his hands:

> 'This typical workman's gesture made me so dizzy that I thought I was falling straight down to a period – or region of myself – long since forgotten. My heart awoke, and at once my body thawed. With wild speed and precision the boy registered on me: his gestures, his hair, the jerk of his hips, the curve of his back, the merry-go-round on which he was working, the movement of the horses, the music, the fair-ground, the city of Antwerp containing them, the Earth cautiously turning, the Universe protecting so precious a burden, and I standing there, frightened at possessing the world and at knowing I possessed it.
> 'I did not see the spit on his hands: I recognised the puckering of the cheek and the tip of the tongue between his teeth. I again saw the boy rubbing his tough, black palms. As he bent down to grab the handle, I noticed his cracked, but thick leather belt. A belt of that kind could not be an ornament like the one that holds up the trousers of a man of fashion. By its material and thickness it was penetrated with the

---

[2] William Burroughs, *The Soft Machine* (1970)

following function: holding up the most obvious sign of masculinity which, without the strap, would be nothing, would no longer contain, would no longer guard its manly treasure but would tumble down on the heels of a shackled male. The boy was wearing a windcheater, between which and the trousers could be seen his skin. As the belt was not inserted into loops, at every movement it rose a bit as the trousers slid down. I stared at the belt, spellbound. I saw it operating surely. At the sixth jerk of the hips, it girdled – except at the fly, where the two ends were buckled – the chap's bare back and waist.'[3]

Note that there is not a single 'offensive' word or phrase in the paragraph, yet the urgency of the narrator's sudden flare of desire is perfectly conveyed by incidental but telling and significant detail. The word 'offensive', incidentally, is an important one in this context. The extracts from Miller and Burroughs present an interesting test: you may personally be repelled by Miller's chauvinism and brutality, or by Burroughs' homosexuality, but if you find the passages I have quoted 'offensive', if you find the language itself objectionable, you are not cut out to write erotic books! You may not yourself care to write such scenes; but you must be capable of understanding that some people, somewhere, find such scenes erotic, and must not be castigated for doing so. The freedom to give offence is as much the right of an erotic author as of a political journalist, and in the nature of things likely to be more frequently exercised.

Writing erotica for money

The American writer Anaïs Nin (1903-1977) is probably the best-known woman writer of erotic prose of our time. Reading the remarkable stories in her collections *Delta of Venus* and *Little Birds*, we can only guess whether she would ever have expressed her interest in sex and sexuality quite so overtly if (as she wrote in the preface to *Delta of Venus*) she had not been particularly hard up when in 1940 Henry Miller told her of a book collector who had offered him $100 a month to write erotic stories for a rich client. She arranged to write for this anonymous man – who she never met: they communicated by telephone.

'Today I received a telephone call. A voice said, "It is fine. But leave out the poetry and description of anything but sex. Concentrate on sex." So I began to write tongue-in-cheek, to become outlandish, inventive, and so exaggerated that I thought he would realise I was caricaturing sexuality. But there was no protest. I spent days

[3] Jean Genet, *The Thief's Journal* (1949)

in the library studying the *Kama Sutra*, listened to friends' most extreme adventures.

' "Less poetry," said the voice over the telephone. "Be specific." But did anyone ever experience pleasure from reading a clinical description? Didn't the old man know how words carry colours and sounds into the flesh?. . .

'This started an epidemic of erotic "journals". Everyone was writing up their sexual experiences. Invented, overheard, researched from Krafft-Ebing and medical books. We had comical conversations. We told a story and the rest of us had to decide whether it was true or false. Or plausible. Was this plausible? Robert Duncan would offer to experiment, to test our inventions, to confirm or negate our fantasies. All of us needed money, so we pooled our stories. . .'

Later the client seemed to broaden his appetite, so

'I gathered poets around me and we all wrote beautiful erotica. As we were condemned to focus only on sensuality, we had violent explosions of poetry. Writing erotica became a road to sainthood rather than to debauchery. . . The homosexuals wrote as if they were women. The timid ones about frenzied fulfilments. The most poetic ones indulged in pure bestiality and the purest ones in perversions. . .'

Anaïs Nin's erotic writing is more often than not excellent: despite her own reservations, it is usually psychologically true, often extremely atmospheric, and assaults the sensitivities neither of women or men. Men, and not only male writers, could learn a lot by reading her short stories – and perhaps have done so. In *The Basque and Bijou*, included in the anthology *The Delta of Venus* (1969), she writes of a happy sexual experience at a brothel – satisfactory not only for the man, but for the prostitute, often misused by men:

'The gluttony of other men, their egotism, their eagerness to satisfy themselves without appreciation of her, made her hostile. But the Basque was gallant. He compared her skin to satin, her hair to moss, her odour to the scent of precious woods. Then he placed his sex at the opening and said tenderly: "Does it hurt? I won't push it in if it hurts."

'Such delicacy moved Vivian. She said, "It hurts just a little, but try."

'He advanced only half an inch at a time. "Does it hurt?" He offered to take it out. Then Vivian had to press him. "Just the tip. Try again"

'So the tip slipped in an inch or two, then rested. This gave Vivian plenty of time in which to feel its presence, time that other men did not give her. Between each tiny advance into her, she had leisure to feel how pleasant its presence was between the soft walls of flesh, how well it fitted, neither too tight nor too loose. Again he waited, then advanced a little more. Vivian had time to feel how good it was to be filled, how well suited the female crevice was to hold and to keep. The pleasure of having something to hold there, exchanging warmth, mingling the two moistures. He moved again. The suspense. The awareness of the emptiness when he withdrew – her flesh withered almost immediately. She closed her eyes. His gradual entrance threw radiations all around it, invisible currents warning the deeper regions of her womb that some explosion was coming, something made to fit in the soft-walled tunnel and to be devoured by its hungry depths, where restless nerves lay waiting. Her flesh yielded more and more. He entered further. . .

'The flesh walls moved like sea anemones, seeking by suction to draw his sex in, but it was only near enough to sent currents of excruciating pleasure. He moved again, watching her face. Then he saw her mouth open. She wanted to raise her body now, to take his sex in wholly, but she waited. By this slow teasing he had her on the edge of hysteria. She opened her mouth as if to reveal the openness of her womb, its hunger, and only then did he plunge to the very bottom and felt her contractions.'[4]

Can there be any serious objection to such a scene, so sensitively written? Does it not have too a tenderness which makes it, despite the setting, an expression of *loving* sex? (There is similar example on p.30)

Improper or 'unnecessary'?

One can understand objections to Miller (on the grounds that he degrades women) and Burroughs (on the grounds of his violence and 'perversion'); one can understand objections to the republication of the novels of the Marquis de Sade – though whether they should actually be banned is another and more contentious matter. But objections to such a scene as Ms Nin's are more difficult to advance; they usually consist, in the end, of the suggestion that it is in some way improper or 'unnecessary' to accompany characters beyond the bedroom door (or, these days, to the floor of the living-room, beneath the shower, or almost anywhere else). At a Cheltenham Literary Festival during the year when John Braine's *Room at the Top* had been published and he was a guest in the town, I overheard two elderly ladies in conversation:

'Have you read it?'

'No – it's all about sex, you know; and one gets enough of that at home.'

Setting aside the obvious good luck of the lady concerned, here is an argument which seems from the first to be ridiculous. The answer to the question 'Why write about sex?' can only be a simple 'Why not?' It is as much a part of life as eating, breathing, working. And of course what the puritans forget is that it has always

---

[4] Anaïs Nin, *The Delta of Venus* (1978)

been with us, in or out of disguise, consciously or unconsciously, recognised or unrecognised. Fairy stories and nursery rhymes are a case in point: Victorian ladies who were so delighted to read and recite them to their children would have been less delighted had they realised the implications of the details in such tales as that of Cinderella, whose shoe was not of glass but of fur (the confusion arose, no doubt, because the story is a French one, and the French for 'glass' is *verre*). The implication is obvious, as it is with the 'kiss' that awakened the Sleeping Beauty.

So if we cannot argue that erotic writing is the product of a filthy modern age, that it is always harmful, always degrading to women, always unnecessary in fiction – where are we? I would suggest that we need to consider whether, if pornography is the product of violent male chauvinism and obscenity often the adult version of schoolboy scatology, truly erotic writing is not (or should not be) the healthy and tender result of natural sexual fantasy – of an appetite which, like other appetites, needs not only physical but emotional nurture.

3
Historical erotic fiction

There is only a limited amount of specific advice to offer to writers who want to write erotic fiction: the rules which apply to fiction in general also apply to it, though in some cases (of plotting, for instance) less forcibly. There are several books which can be of help in that respect – among them some in the same series as this title.

Of course it is true that every aspiring novelist should familiarise herself with fiction in general; and this rule applies equally to erotic literature. But there is the difficulty that being 'disreputable' it is not in general taught in schools, and must be sought out. Many classic erotic works are now available in paperback; others are not – the great omission is Jack Saul's two-volume *The Sins of the Cities of the Plain* (1881) which is a riveting and believable portrait of the Victorian homosexual underworld (Saul was a protagonist in the notorious Cleveland Street affair, which involved the then heir to the throne of England, Prince Eddy).

For someone living outside the larger cities, tracking down the erotica of the past is not easy. Frequently it is difficult to know where to look for it, and it is often difficult to find when one *does* know where to look. The British Library and the university libraries now at least no longer keep their pornography locked away in special cupboards (the Private Case at the British Museum was notorious for generations before its books were made freely available to serious scholars). But there is no separate catalogue of erotica, so you have to know the titles or authors of the books you may want to read. There is now what amounts to a catalogue of the erotica in the British Library – Patrick J. Kearney's *The Private Case* (1981); and my selective bibliography may also be a help.

In the meantime, here is a brief history of erotic literature in English, with a number of quotations which give the flavour of the various periods, and will direct the reader to particular areas which it might be profitable for him or her to explore further. The history of literary censorship falls outside my scope, but for sheer comedy and a display of hypocrisy I cannot too strong advise everyone interested in the subject to read C. H. Rolph's *The Trial of Lady Chatterley* and Tony Palmer's *The Trials of Oz* (1971).

Early days

For some centuries, erotic books published in England appeared only in languages unlikely to be understood by the common reader. Not that there were many common readers, but just as, later, censorship by price attempted to ensure that 'curious books' were kept out of the hands of those people too poor to possess them (and therefore unlikely to be sufficiently educated to appreciate them), so – as with the Bible – the fact that a book was published only in Latin similarly guaranteed that only the learned could read it – and as Mr Griffith-Jones was to point out (see p.9) one's wife or servant would not be in danger of corruption. As soon as man set pen to paper brief erotic squibs, in verse and prose, were written down. These were in the main simple jokes, like the Anglo-Saxon monks' riddles which were the equivalent of twentieth century schoolboy smut, and which were 'published' mainly by being circulated in the form of written notes and by word of mouth. And in the earliest days when books were available in English, sexual passages were printed without any difficulties with the authorities. In 1566, for instance, William Aldington published a translation of Apuleius' novel *The Transformation of Lucius Apuleius* (better known as *The Golden Ass*) which included passages which the Victorians were to find unprintable – Apuleius' account of his affair with Fotis, a slave-girl, for instance:

> 'When I had well replenished myself with wine, and was now ready unto venery not only in mind but also in body, I removed my clothes, and showing to Fotis my great impatience I said, "O my sweet heart, take pity upon me and help me, for as you see I am now prepared unto the battle which you yourself did appoint - for after that I felt the arrow of cruel Cupid within my breast, I bent my bow very strong, and now fear (because it is bended so hard) lest my string should break; but that thou mayest the better please me, undress thy hair and come and embrace me lovingly." Whereupon she made no long delay, but set aside all the meat and wine, and then she unapparelled herself, and unattired her hair, presenting her amiable body unto me in manner of fair Venus when she goeth under the waves of the sea. "Now," quoth she, "is come the hour of jousting; now is come the time of war, wherefore show thyself like unto a man, for I will not retire, I will not fly the field. See then thou be valiant; see thou be courageous, since there is no time appointed when our skirmish shall cease." In saying these words she came to me to bed, and embraced

me sweetly, and so we passed all the night in pastime and pleasure, and never slept until it was day: but we would eftsoons refresh our weariness, and provoke our pleasure, and renew our venery by drinking of wine. In which sort we pleasantly passed away many other nights following.'

Here are a number of devices still happily in use today: the eagerness of the man (compared to the eagerness of a warrior impatient for battle), the sly simile (the bent bow compared to the strength of the penis), the eagerness of the woman, and the night-long pleasure – and all without a single 'offensive' word.

Daphnis and Chloe

Almost a century later, George Thornley made another translation, from the Latin, of Longus. *Pastoral Matters concerning Daphnis and Chloe* is one of the earliest examples of a classic in which the erotic content is so spirited that the author could almost have been accused of writing pornography. The two young innocents, Daphnis and Chloe, are in love but completely ignorant of sex – until a neighbour's young wife, Lycaenium, fancying Daphnis, offers to demonstrate the pleasures – at which point Daphnis

'throwes himself at the foot of Lycaenium and begs of her That she would teach him quickly that Art by which he should be able, as he would, to do Chloe. . . Wherefore Lycaenium now she had found the Goat-herd so willing and forward beyond her expectation, began to instruct the Lad thus – She bid him sit down as near to her as possibly he could, and that he should kisse her as close and as often as he used to kisse Chloe; and while he kist her to clip her in his arms and hugg her to him, and lye down with her upon the ground. As now he was sitting, and kissing, and lay down with her; She, when she saw him itching to be at her, lifted him up from the reclination on his side, and slipping under, not without art, directed him to her Fancie, the place so long desired and sought. Of that which happened after this, there was nothing done that was strange, nothing that was insolent: the Lady Nature and Lycaenium shewed him how to do the rest. . .'

The initiation of an innocent – male or female – has often been similarly described, and succeeds no doubt not only because of the traditional pleasure men take in the idea of making love to a virgin, but because the fresh, previously untried pleasure of a good first sexual experience always seems enviable. Here too is the trick of drawing the veil at the climactic moment. But note how language is changing: the word 'do' makes a very early appearance for 'fuck', and 'fancie' for 'cunt' – and these are erotic without being obscene.

These are examples of literature, the equivalent of the modern 'serious' novel in which sex appears only as a part of the whole – an important part, but only a part.

L'Ecole des Filles

Book-length erotica in English – that is, books written simply and entirely to 'amuse' by describing sexual encounters – began to circulate in England in the middle of the seventeenth century, most of it written by foreigners, and much of it still only published in the original language. A prime example was *L'Ecole des filles*, first published in the original French by Michel Millot and Jean L'Ange in 1655. Within ten years of its publication it came into England via Holland and a copy was picked up in London on January 13, 1668 by Samuel Pepys. Apparently in all innocence, he dropped in at Martin's, his bookseller's, to find a French book 'for my wife to translate' (she was a Huguenot); but 'when I came to look in it, it is the most bawdy, lewd book that ever I saw. . . so that I was ashamed of reading in it, and so away home'.   Nevertheless, he returned later 'and bought the idle, roguish book *L'escholle des filles*' and carried it off in plain covers – later noting in his diary that while it was undoubtedly lewd, it was 'not amiss for a sober man to read over to inform himself in the villainy of the world.' Later the same evening he re-read it, masturbated, then burned the book 'that it might not be among my books to my shame.'

It was not long before the book appeared in English and by 1688 booksellers were being prosecuted for selling *The School of Venus*. It is an early example of a *genre* which has subsequently been much used: an 'educational' book in which the authors imagined an experienced girl explaining to a naive friend the pleasures and pains of sex. It is not ill done: the characters are by no means simply lay figures and the situations have some psychological truth.

Fanny (in the English version) has been enthusing to her younger and more innocent friend Katy about the joys of love, and the latter has decided that she can no longer do without them. Happily, a Mr Roger (the pun was no doubt intentional) is available, and Katy's description of his first approach to her is entirely believable, with considerable uncontrived psychological truth (I quote from the earliest translation; there have been many since):

> 'When he came into the chamber, he saluted me and asked me how I did. I made him a civil answer and desired him to sit down, which he soon did close by me, staring me full in the face, and all quivering and shaking asked me if my mother was at home, and told me he met you at the bottom of the stairs and that you had spoken to him about me, desiring to know if it were with my consent. I returning no answer,

but smiled, he grew bolder and immediately kissed me, which I
permitted without struggling, tho' it made me blush as red as fire for
the resolution I had taken to let him do what he would do unto me.
He took notice of it and said, "What do you blush for, child? Come,
kiss me again." In doing of which he was longer than usual, and
thrusted his tongue into my mouth. 'Tis a folly to lie, that way of
kissing pleased me, that if I had not before received your instructions
I should have granted him whatever he demanded. . . I received his
tongue under mine, which he riggled about, then he stroked my
neck, sliding his hand under my handkerchief he handled my
breasts, thrusting his hands as low as he could. . .'

This all sounds like a young girl talking; and while there
are plenty of descriptions of the mechanics of sex, the personal
tone persists:

'After a little pause he got up his breeches and sat down by me,
told me he should be bound unto you so long as he lived, how
he met you at the stairs' foot, where with your good news you
rejoiced the very soul of him, for without such tidings the agony
he was in for the love of me would certainly have killed him, that
the love which he had so long had for me encouraged him to be
doing, but that he wanted boldness and rhetorick to tell me his
mind, that he wanted words to express my deserts, which he found
since he enjoyed me to be beyond his imagination. And therefore he
resolved to make a friendship with me as lasting as his life, with a
hundred protestations of services he would do me, entreating me
still to love him and be true unto him, promising the like on his
part, and that he would have no friendship for any woman else,
and that he would every day come and fuck me twice. For these
compliments I made him a low curtsy and gave him thanks with
all my heart. He then plucked out of his pockets some pistachios,
which he gave me to eat, telling me it was the best restorative in
the world after fucking.'

This is far from being the sixteenth century predecessor of the
underground pulp Victorian sex shocker. The characterisation may
be vestigial, but there is enough of it to make the reader believe in
the people concerned and there are several delightful comic
touches – like the pistachios – which lightens the tone. In fact, much
of the book is a pleasure to read for its own sake; the fact that Mr
Roger is no more honest than the hero of any other similar tale is
beside the point and indeed contributes to the erotic tension. We all
know what is likely to happen over the page, and happen it does,
Katy's task, as far as the reader is concerned, being to learn still
more about the pleasures of love and the delights the male anatomy
can hold:

I now began to be more familiar with it than before and took a great deal of satisfaction with holding it in my hand, measuring the length and breadth of it, wondering at the virtue it had to please us so strangely. . .

And so on.

L'Académie des Dames

By this time there were other similar books available in English: a translation for instance of *L'Académie des Dames*, which came out in 1688 as *A Dialogue between a Married Lady and a Maid*. The French book was said to be a translation of one by a Spanish woman, Luisa Sigea – but it seems more likely to have been written by its French 'translator', Nicolas Chorier (b.1609). It is far less affable than *The School of Venus;* the sex is rougher, the tone much more chauvinistic. The lesson to be learned from it is that the best erotica (as opposed, of course, to the best *writing* about sex) is fantasy: everything is always for the best in the best of all possible beds; there is no disease, no unwanted pregnancy and rape is a game.

Yes, of course in real life rape is never a game; but neither are we free from the risks of unprotected sex. In erotic fiction, however, it is another matter. Realism is very often counterproductive. No male reader would particularly want to be reminded, for instance, of the embarrassment of premature ejaculation; Chorier presents this not merely as an embarrassment to Caviceo, his hero, but as repulsive to Ottavia, his mistress, who cries:

> 'Unlucky event! – I found myself completely drenched with a regular shower like fire, and, naked as I was, wet up to the navel. I put my hand to [his lance] again; but, when falling on that sort of slimy fluid with which the mad fellow had flooded me, my hand recoiled with fright and horror.'

Fright and horror may have their place in a novel, even in an erotic novel. But revulsion is another matter. Chorier also shows himself in some sense to be a puritan: while he advocates libertinism, this is true only up to a point. He allows his character Tullia to describe in detail every possible gymnastic coital position, but (having been thoroughly enthusiastic in describing lesbian activities) also delivers through her lips a lecture on the atrocity of male homosexuality, which 'deserves every species of torture and reprobation' (sodomy was of course at that time a capital offence). *The Dialogue* and *The School of Venus* were foreign products, and many other translations were published during the seventeenth century, including *Venus in the Cloyster*, which played an important part in the development of the English law on obscene publication. The Englishman we have to thank for the first native book of erotica is that curious fellow John Wilmot, the second Earl of Rochester (1647-80). He was a poet who wrote some wonderful love poems, but whose full-length play *Sodom, or the Quintessence of Debauchery* is about as subtle as its author's public behaviour (he was once seen drunk, on a balcony, with equally inebriated cronies, pissing upon the people walking below). A number of his poems were circulated during his lifetime but not published until 1963, when a Yale professor produced a complete edition.

There is not a great deal to be learned from most of his erotic poems, which are often so crude and obscene that sensuality is about the last emotion likely to be aroused by them. What is regrettable is that rather than taking the easy way out (by writing cheap verse in which as many scatological references as possible could be crowded) he did not give some thought to how poetry could be made genuinely erotic – he had both the poetical equipment and the emotional sensitivity to do this, witness his wonderful *Song of a Young Lady to her Ancient Lover* (see p.91).

Fanny Hill

As far as erotic literature was concerned there was something of a hiatus at the end of the seventeenth century. However, in 1748-9 came an enormously important event: the publication of the first true erotic novel written in English, which remains still one of the best, John Cleland's *The Memoirs of a Woman of Pleasure*, which we know better as *Fanny Hill*. This was only now possible, for it was only in the 1740s that, substantially, the novel form was 'invented' (by Samuel Richardson, the author of *Pamela*).

Cleland was born in 1709, educated at Westminster School, and as a young man served as British consul at Smyrna. After working for some time in Bombay, for the East India Company, he returned to England and staved off poverty by what means he could. Indeed, it was while he was in prison for debt that he wrote a manuscript which he sold to a publisher, Ralph Griffiths, for twenty guineas. *The Memoirs of a Woman of Pleasure* came out in 1749, and was to make Griffiths a profit of ten thousand pounds. At first he was threatened with prosecution for publishing it, and hastily put out a bowdlerised version in two volumes, which was rather well received, at least by a critic in *The Monthly Review*. Though originally it had been (wrote the reviewer) 'a very loose work', it was rather moral:

'Vice has indeed fair quarter allowed it; and after painting whatever charms it may pretend to boast, with the fairest impartiality, the supposed female writer concludes with a lively declaration in favour of sobriety, temperance and virtue, on even the mere considerations of a life of *true taste* and happiness in *this world*. . .'

The prosecution was dropped.

The main point to be made about Cleland's book, one of the reasons for its success, and certainly something to be kept in mind by all writers of erotic fiction, is that it celebrated both lust and love. Fanny certainly had her trials; but through them all she remained constant in spirit to her first lover Charles, with whom she achieved a happy matrimonial conclusion. The book ends, interestingly enough, with a plea for sex education: when their son reaches the proper age, Charles himself

> 'led him by the hand thro' the most noted bawdy-houses in town, where he took care he should be familiarized with all those scenes of debauchery. . . The experiment, you will cry, is dangerous? True, on a fool; but are fools worth so much attention?'

Quite apart from Cleland's moral attitude, he was a better writer than any that had so far attempted erotic prose in English. He also had the advantage of being able very convincingly to imagine himself as a woman – necessary, because his book is narrated by Fanny herself, a country girl who recalls her adventures in a letter to an unknown female recipient. The book is remarkably free of sadism, and while it presents various forms of sexual preference without criticism, and with what seems a charming curiosity (Fanny is particularly amused by the elderly gentleman whose pleasure is to give her innumerable pairs of gloves, which she must put on before he bites off the finger-ends) it never criticises and never condemns. Indeed, one of the interesting episodes in it is astonishing for its time: Fanny looks on as two young men enjoy sodomy, her only criticism being that the penis of the active partner is 'an engine that certainly deserved to be put to a better use'. In addition, Cleland makes a point of emphasising the 'tender, long-breathed kiss' exchanged by the partners. In other words, the act was not presented with the repulsion with which the law then regarded it, though Fanny does emphasise that sodomy is 'a criminal act', and went about to report it (presumably to the authorities), but unfortunately fell down and the culprits escaped. There is little doubt that such condemnation as Cleland did express through Fanny was inserted only for appearances, and indeed the book seems to contain evidence that the female side of Cleland's personality was sufficiently marked to enable him to see her erotic life through Fanny's eyes and senses. Indeed, one of the finest passages in the book is a description by her of her lover, as she wakes by his side on the morning after he has deflowered her:

'Oh! could I paint his figure, as I see it now, still present to my transported imagination! a whole length of an all-perfect, manly beauty in full view. Think of a face without a fault, glowing with all the opening bloom and vernal freshness of an age in which beauty is of either sex, and which the first down over his upper lip scarce began to distinguish.

'The parting of the double ruby pout of his lips seem'd to exhale an air sweeter and purer than what it drew in: ah! what violence did it not cost me to refrain the so tempted kiss!

'Then a neck exquisitely turn'd, grac'd behind and on the sides with his hair, playing freely in natural ringlets, connected his head to a body of the most perfect form, and of the most vigorous contexture, in which all the strength of manhood was conceal'd and soften'd to appearance by the delicacy of his complexion, the smoothness of his skin, and the plumpness of his flesh.

'The platform of his snow-white bosom, that was laid out in a manly proportion, presented, on the vermilion summit of each pap, the idea of a rose abut to blow.

'Nor did his shirt hinder me from observing that symmetry of his limbs, that exactness of shape, in the fall of it towards the loins, where the waist ends and the rounding swell of the hips commences; where the skin, sleek, smooth, and dazzling white, burnishes on the stretch over firm, plump, ripe flesh, that crimp'd and ran into dimples at the least pressure, or that the touch could not rest upon, but slid over as on the surface of the most polished ivory.

'His thighs, finely fashioned, and with a florid glossy roundness, gradually tapering away to the knees, seem'd pillars worthy to support that beauteous frame; at the bottom of which I could not, without some remains of terror, some tender emotions too, fix my eyes on that terrible machine, which had, not long before, with such fury broke into, torn, and almost ruin'd those soft, tender parts of mine that had not yet done smarting with the effects of its rage; but behold it now! crest fall'n, reclining its half-capt vermilion head over one of his thighs, quiet, pliant, and to all appearance incapable of the mischiefs and cruelty it had committed. The beautiful growth of the hair, in short and soft curls round its root, its whiteness, branch'd veins, the supple softness of the shaft, as it lay foreshorten'd, roll'd and shrunk up into a squab thickness, languid, and borne up between his thighs by its globular appendage, that wondrous treasure-bag of nature's sweets, which, rivell'd round, and purs'd up in the only wrinkles that are known to please, perfected the prospect, and all together formed the most interesting moving picture in nature, and surely infinitely superior to those nudities furnish'd by the painters, statuaries, or any art, which are purchased at immense prices. . .'

It is interesting that this passage is a description by a heterosexual male author of a male character – and is as an enthusiastic a portrait, as observant and celebratory of male beauty, as any woman writer or gay man could achieve. It underlines the fact that erotic fiction is no place for homophobia. It also underlines what I have already said: the writer of erotic books must be prepared to free his female (or her male) instincts from the straitjacket in which twentieth century inhibition may have confined them. It is no surprise that those Victorian men who so freely cried in public, and who could write as openly about their emotional commitments to their male friends as Tennyson did in *In Memoriam*, were capable of writing good erotic prose.

Fanny's description of her lover not only makes the reader understand their relationship more completely (Charles remains, throughout her many amorous adventures, the one partner she really loves, and with whom – therefore – her pleasure is greatest) but makes us believe more thoroughly in her as a woman whose sexual appetite is both voracious and wholesome. No-one reading that passage, I suggest, could have any doubt that Fanny's pleasures are wholehearted and uninhibited (seeing Charles, the bedclothes thrown off, she 'hung over him enamour'd indeed! and devoured all his naked charms with only two eyes, when I could have wish'd them at least a hundred for the fuller enjoyment of the gaze').

Romance and humour

Then, there is the language. Anaïs Nin, who argued for more poetry in pornography, must have admired *Fanny Hill* – not only for its romanticism (the boy's nipples reminding Fanny of 'a rose about to blow. . .') but for the charming humour of 'the only wrinkles that are known to please' and of the 'terrible machine' reduced to something 'incapable of the mischiefs and cruelty it had committed' (though waking, Charles rapidly proved that his condition was only temporary). And, romanticism and humour apart, there remains a description of male beauty that is almost tangible.

In a sense, it is easy to write such a passage in such a manner; no-one would be likely, I suppose, to find the paragraphs I have quoted offensive. But how did Cleland deal with action, especially in scenes which it would be easy to make crude and raw? The answer is that he used humour – to an extent rare in twentieth century erotic writing:

[A young foreigner's] 'red-headed champion, that has so lately fled the pit, quell'd and abash'd, was now recover'd to the top of his condition,

perk'd and crested up between Polly's thighs, who was not wanting,
on her part, to coax and keep it in good humour, stroking it, with her
head down, and received even its velvet tip between the lips of not its
proper mouth: whether she did this out of any particular pleasure, or
whether it was to render it more glib and easy of entrance, I could not
tell; but it had such an effect, that the young gentleman seem'd by
his eyes, that sparkled with more excited lustre, and his inflamed
countenance, to receive increase of pleasure. He got up, and taking
Polly in his arms, embraced her, and said something too softly for me
to hear, leading her withal to the foot of the couch, and taking delight
to slap her thighs and posteriors with that stiff sinew of his, which
hit them with a spring that he gave it with his hand, and made them
resound again, but hurt her about as much as he meant to hurt her, for
she seemed to have as frolic a taste as himself.

'But guess my surprise, when I saw the lazy young rogue lie down
upon his back, and gently pull down Polly upon him, who giving way
to his humour, straddled, and with her hands conducted her blind
favourite to the right place; and following her impulse, ran directly
upon the flaming point of this weapon of pleasure, which she stak'd
herself upon, up pierc'd, in infix'd to the extremest hair-breadth of it:
thus she sat on him a few instants, enjoying and relishing her situation,
whilst he toyed with her provoking breasts. Sometime she would stoop
to meet his kiss: but presently the sting of pleasure spurr'd them up
to fiercer action; then began the storm of heaves, which, from the
undermost combatant, were thrusts at the same time, he crossing his
hands over her, and drawing her home to him with a sweet violence;
the inverted strokes of anvil over hammer soon brought on the critical
period, in which all the sighs of a close conspiring extasy informed us
of the point they were at.'

It is easy (and to some extent reasonable) to argue that it is the
language of Cleland's period that charms us, that makes such
passages seem somehow softer, more loving and more humourous
than a similar modern passage would be likely to be. Well, of course
we tend to be seduc'd by the language. But the effect is stronger
than that: it was not only Cleland's skill as a writer, but his whole
attitude that informs his work. It is an attitude the twentieth century
writer of erotic prose will do well to note and emulate.

Restif de la Bretonne

In France however it was another matter. The work of Restif de la
Bretonne (1734-1806) could scarcely have been commended from
any pulpit. He set out to write an enormous erotic novel of round
about 1,500 pages, entitled *L'Anti-Justine*, which may or may not
ever have been finished. It began to appear in separate volumes in
France in 1863 (a rough and ready translation of parts of it was

published in English, in Paris, in 1895, under the title *The Double Life of Cuthbert Cockerton*).

Restif claimed that his book was to be the antithesis of the Marquis de Sade's 'foul performances'. De Sade's *Justine, ou les Malheurs de la vertu,* had been published in 1791, and like his other books, displayed a polymorphous perversity unequalled in pornography. Whatever his virtues as a novelist, they are non-existent as far as erotic writing is concerned – the general reader is surely unlikely to be sexually aroused by his novels – more likely, one would think, to be put off sex for life.

While Restif thoroughly abhorred de Sade's books, and said that he 'wished to write a book more sweet to the taste than any of de Sade's, which wives could present to their lazy husbands with the hope of better results', his *Anti-Justine* has its own extremes of perversity. There are few novels in which incest is more pervasive; necrophilia and cannibalism also play their part, and 'sweeter' is scarcely the word one would apply to the book, even by comparison to the Marquis' work.

Of more interest to us is Restif's autobiography, *Monsieur Nicolas, or the Human Heart Laid Bare.* By the time he was sixty he had published four volumes and planned twelve more. He actually completed this enormous task by 1797. His book is one of the most remarkable autobiographies ever published, with fascinating detail of village and city life in nineteenth century France. It is very sad that it has never been published in its entirety in English translation: a single volume of extracts translated by Robert Baldick was published in 1966. *M Nicolas* certainly seriously rivals Casanova's autobiography, which covers the years 1725-85 and was first published in 1838 (though an unexpurgated text only appeared in English in 1961).

Here is true autobiography – the description of Bretonne as 'the chambermaids' Voltaire' and 'the Rousseau of the gutter' is unfair; he was admired by readers as disparate as Beaumarchais and Goethe. This is a splendidly vivid account of Restif's adventures as a young man in search of sex. Even when he was like most young men inconsiderate or even cruel, the saving graces of humour and a real talent for narrative make his book sympathetic, while he conveys his sensual pleasures vividly enough to involve his readers. He also had the advantage of never being ashamed of his adventures: a lack of shame is entirely necessary to the erotic autobiographer – nothing is less aphrodisiac than any suggestion that the writer *and his lovers* did not enjoy themselves.

Restif, interestingly, does not go into great detail – but because he is so good a narrator of situation and character, he manages to convey a high erotic charge without the necessity for physiological detail.

Staying at a house in Paris, he manages to seduce the chambermaid:

> 'I tried to obtain the favours of Thérèse Courbisson,' he writes.
> 'I succeeded; the young girl was no prude. Our meetings took place
> on the cellar stairs, when she went to fetch the wine for supper.'

Because we have previously been introduced so vividly to little Thérèse, because we know the house, and the stairs – and M. Richecoeur, who discovers Restif and the girl *in flagrante* – the situation is real and intense and as effective as if the writer had spent four pages describing the minutiae of their encounter. Indeed throughout *Monsieur Nicolas* he shows this kind of restraint and it makes the often farcical situations into which he gets himself as effective, in a different way, as any microscopic depiction of what went on. But then, the subtitle of his book is *The Human Heart Laid Bare*, and he was as interested in the psychological truth of a situation (though he would not have put it in those terms) as in physical accuracy.

Casanova's memoirs

Though the general impression is probably otherwise, Jacopo Casanova did not often go into over-literal detail in his celebrated diaries. He is more self-conscious than Restif, and nowhere near as good a writer. With him it was the adventures – or perhaps fantasies – that mattered rather than the manner of setting them down – but he was a considerably more flamboyant and of course better-known character, and manages to convey his enthusiasm without making the reader pause to consider what an unpleasant fellow he was. When he writes of being in bed with two young women there is no question of the reader pausing to wonder about the morality of the situation; Casanova manages to take one with him, as it were, and while he does not hesitate to compare the two girls in general terms, his description of what followed could be read without offence by the most energetic puritan.

When he does go into clinical detail it is less from a desire to arouse than out of simple interest, which he cannot resist conveying to his reader: 'I would really never have thought that anything could have distracted me from the pleasure of holding naked in my arms the body of a woman I loved', he writes – but has to pause when he notices that another girl who happens to be in the same bed at the time with her companion, has a particularly large clitoris. 'Goodness,' (he seems to say) 'isn't *that* interesting!' – but then carries on with the business in hand.

Restif's is the earliest autobiography celebrated for such sexual frankness that it is of interest to readers (and writers) of erotic prose. He set out to be completely frank about himself – more frank, he asserts, than St Augustine or Rousseau – and as far as one can judge, fulfilled the ambition. Though quite a large proportion of the book is occupied by his sexual adventures, a great deal of it (as with *M. Nicolas*) simply records everyday life. The result of this mixture is that the erotic passages come alive with that kind of graphic colour lacking in other simply pornographic works in which there is little light and shade, and are far more strongly erotic than anything in *Anti-Justine*, for instance. Restiv's honesty extends to various misfortunes as well as to revealing himself as an enthusiastic shoe-fetishist; he is not without humour – there is an hilarious lesson in the results of reading pornographic literature, when as the result of dipping into an erotic book he becomes so inflamed that he tumbles six girls in quick succession. It is possible – no, no – probable that he is fabricating rather than boasting, but the result is a passage which is comic as well as erotic, a *coup* not easy to achieve.

The point is that Restif produced an autobiography which is a great deal more readable than Casanova's, and a great deal more sympathetic than the two English autobiographies which, written in the following century, stand with it: those of 'Walter' and Frank Harris.

Walter's secret life

My Secret Life, by 'Walter', is about the same length as Restif's book. It was written in the 1890s and published by the author in an edition of only six copies of eleven volumes, totalling 4,200 pages. It remains perhaps the frankest sexual autobiography ever written, and its frankness is its downfall as a successful erotic book. 'Walter' confesses all, and especially to a reader with late twentieth century susceptibilities, all is a great deal too much. Even most pae-dophiles would perhaps be shocked by his account of buying a small girl from a woman in Vauxhall Gardens: 'She had an anxious look as she stared at me', he writes, adding after he had pleasured himself, 'She did not holler at all, really.' Having made love – no, that is the wrong word; having fucked a young woman he later discovers to be pregnant, he describes her as a slut, and then remarks 'It was an exciting termination to the day.'

The trouble with the book, apart from Walter's own animal nature, is not that it seems to have been written with the same urgency as that which drove him to use so many women to slake a priapic lust, nor that he was completely unashamed of his sexual life, but that he was to us a totally unsympathetic character with whom, I suppose, scarcely a single reader would want to identify. Moreover, he is put into such an excited state by recalling the episodes he sets down, that he exercises no skill at all (and he is not so good a writer that felicities come unbidden). He simply sets down what happened, without any attempt to convey his own pleasure except in the crudest terms.

He was for instance a determined voyeur, but rarely does more than state the fact. For example, when in a Paris hotel he found himself in the next room to a pretty woman, made a hole in the wall with a pair of scissors, and 'instead of going to see the cathedral and other things I had come to see, I did nothing but watch this lady'. Do we get any idea that he received anything like what we would recognise as pleasure from this, however?

> 'She had luncheon at the hotel. Soon after, up she went, up I went, and quickly saw her pee-wee, and then – oh joy! her husband came in. Then she put herself on the bed side, he turned up her clothes, contemplated her for a minute (and so did I), and after a minute, he shagged her. There was not much ceremony between the two, they both wanted it, very very quick about it, and enjoyed it. Then they both went out, and she never washed. I should have heard the basin if she had.'

Such passages certainly convince one that Walter's book is a genuine autobiography: what would be the purpose of writing such a paragraph if it were not? But it is certainly not erotic – and few of his pages are.

The lesson of all this is that if you choose the autobiographical form for an erotic book (supposing that you have led a sex-life sufficiently *mouvementé*) you must be prepared to distance yourself from the sexual episodes and consider them in the same light as any other incidents you are recording. You cannot afford to jot them down *ad lib* – you are writing a book, not recording an incident on a lavatory wall. Despite what anyone says about it, erotic prose is a literary form, which means that both elements must be present: immediacy and (for want of a better word) art.

Frank Harris's 'Life'

Frank Harris (1856-1931), the friend of Oscar Wilde, wrote his long autobiography, *My Life and Loves*, right at the end of his life simply to make money. He attempted to ensure its financial success by spicing it not only with innumerable anecdotes, many untrue, about the great and famous, but with equally plentiful amorous interludes – many of which may have been equally untrue, though for one reason or another a number of women willingly conceded that his accounts were accurate.

In some ways, Harris resembles 'Walter'; his sexual manners were far from impeccable. But he was a writer – of some distinction: his biography of Oscar Wilde and his *The Man Shakespeare*, if wilful, are very readable – and when he puts his mind to it, he can certainly write a good erotic scene. In Paris once, as a young man, he picked up a woman, Jeanne, who took him home, where she entertained him with some enthusiasm. With her lived a young girl of about twelve, Lisette, who she had 'adopted' (was Harris being a tad disingenuous, or at least naive?), and who she invited Harris to watch while she was having her bath:

> 'The girl lifted her inscrutable eyes and stood at gaze, a most exquisite picture: the breasts just beginning to be marked, the hips a little fuller than a boy's, the feet and hands smaller – a perfect Tanagra statuette in whitest flesh with a roseate glow on the inside of arms and thighs, while the Mount of Venus was just shadowed with down. She stood there waiting, an entrancing maiden figure. I felt my mouth parching, the pulses in my temples beating. What did it mean? Did Jeanne intend –?'

No doubt Jeanne did intend; Harris, to his credit, did not succumb to temptation (though he allowed himself certain familiarities); it could not be said, I think, that his description does not make the sexual tension of the moment clear.

Professional Victorian pornographers had an enormous commercial success. The Society for the Suppression of Vice reported that in 1834 there were fifty-seven pornographic booksellers in business in Holywell Street alone – selling not only books but magazines, for by the middle of the century there were journals (some short-lived, some surviving for years) to cater for every sexual taste, among them *The Exquisite, Cremorne, The Annals of Gallantry* and *The Englishwoman's Domestic Magazine* (sic!). As literature these were negligible: the best-known is *The Pearl – a Monthly Journal of Facetiae and Voluptuous Reading*, which ran from July 1879 to December 1880 – and has been reprinted in paperback in modern times. Perhaps the most interesting fact to emerge from them is a confirmation of what the French called 'the English vice': flagellation – 'Miss Coote's Confession', in *The Pearl* deals with nothing else.

The English vice

Flagellation has found its way into the work of most erotic writers. Some books deal with nothing else – from *A Treatise on the Use of Flogging* (1718) to *The Thin Lines of Blood* (1989). The earliest books in which the theme was constant were on sale in those brothels –

Mrs Colet's or Mrs Jenkins's or Mrs Berkeley's – which specialised in beating their clients (King George IV visited one). Further down this road we find de Sade and later Leopold von Sacher-Masoch (1836-1895), whose *Venus in Furs* is *the* classic of flagellation and female domination, and who of course gave his name to masochism. His book, written in an extremely luxurious style, has a famous scene in which the heroine, the beautiful widow Wanda van Dunajew, ties up her handsome lover Severin, and, naked except for her furs, whips him.

> '"Just wait, you will yet whine like a dog beneath my whip!" she threatened, and simultaneously began to strike me again.
>
> '"The blows fell quickly, in rapid succession, with terrific force upon my back, arms and neck; I had to grit my teeth not to scream aloud. Now she struck me in the face, warm blood ran down, but she laughed, and continued her blows. . . Never did she seem more seductive to me than today, in spite of all her cruelty and contempt.
>
> '"One step further," commanded Wanda. "Now kneel down, and kiss my foot."
>
> 'She extended her foot beyond the hem of white satin, and I, the supersensual fool, pressed my lips on it.'

Severin finds he enjoys the experience thoroughly – and many readers found that they did, too, with a resulting boom in the sale of whips.

A number of less interesting and certainly less well-written books followed, not only in Germany but elsewhere in Europe. In England some 'respectable' writers turned their hands to the subject – the most famous perhaps being the poet Algernon Charles Swinburne (1837-1909), who contributed a number of pieces to *The Whippingham Papers*, and later included several flagellatory scenes in his novel *Lesbia Brandon*, which largely celebrates Swinburne's twin loves – the birch and the sea. In one scene Denham, a tutor hired to prepare young Bertie for Eton, catches him as he emerges naked from the sea, and punishes him for disobedience:

> 'He took well hold of Bertie, still dripping and blinded; grasped him round the waist and shoulders, wet and naked, with the left arm and laid on with the right as long and as hard as he could. Herbert said afterwards that a wet swishing hurt most awfully; a dry swishing was a comparative luxury. The sting of every cut was doubled or trebled, and he was not released till blood had been drawn from his wet skin, soaked as it was in salt at every pore; and came home at once red and white, drenched and dry.'

No doubt Mr Denham's form of preparation was entirely proper: Eton specialised in beating its boys and this continued well into the present century. Though this was entirely satisfactory, no doubt, for the staff, in adult life outside school it seems to be a fact that more people actually enjoy reading about flagellation than enjoy the act itself – or so several sex surveys have alleged.

To return to the more conventional contents of *The Pearl* and the rest, these are spasmodically genuinely erotic, but the absence for the most part of any kind of literary talent makes them in the end pretty boring. The reader in search of something better turned to Europe – to Casanova or Balzac (whose *Droll Stories* are perhaps 'naughty' rather than really erotic, but are a great deal more readable than *Lady Pokingham, or They All Do It*).

The Moorish Harem

One or two genuine erotic classics were published in England towards the end of the nineteenth century and have remained in print. They are classics at least in the sense that they were widely popular. The best-known is probably *A Night in a Moorish Harem*, a story told by 'Lord George Herbert', said in the Introduction to be the handsomest man in the English Navy, placed in command of one of the finest ships in the fleet at the age of only twenty-three. Having written a description of his interesting adventure, he gave it to 'a fair and frail lady who thought it too good to keep secret', and had it published at her own expense. One hopes it made her a wealthy woman.

It appears that Captain Herbert, his ship at anchor off the Moroccan coast, went for a swim to cool himself, fell asleep in his dinghy, and awoke to find himself drifting near to a high wall down which some pretty women had hung a rope of shawls to assist him to climb to them. An upright Englishman could scarcely resist such an invitation, and in no time our hero is being cosseted by nine inhabitants of a Moorish harem, whose pasha is conveniently away for the night.

No prizes are offered for any suggestion as to what follows, and every delight conceivable by a quite exceptionally virile young man is explored (Herbert asserts that none of the nine women shall go unsatisfied, and is as good as his word). The problem is that the book has no plot: all it has is continual descriptions of copulation, and the reader tires of this considerably before the good Captain. It is one of the lessons to be learned: however good a writer may be at lascivious narrative, something else is needed – something to involve the reader. The only way a book like *A Night in a Moorish Harem* can be enjoyed is in short gasps; it is not the recipe for a good read. (On the other hand, few erotic books do profit from being read at a single gulp).

The Lustful Turk

Rather similar is *The Lustful Turk: a History Founded on Facts, containing an interesting narrative of the cruel fate of two young English ladies named Silvia Carey and Emily Barlow*, which came out first in 1828 and was reprinted again and again during the following seventy years. The book consists of an exchange of letters – a convenient device made popular by such conventional novels as Richardson's *Pamela* and Laclos' *Liaisons Dangereuses* – between the two young ladies in question, prisoners of the Dey of Algiers. The difference between this book and the *Moorish Harem* is in quality: the two girls actually become characters rather than lay figures, though it is still quite clear that the book is written by a man rather than one or even two women. Perhaps the most obvious sign of this is the concentration (to be seen in all Victorian erotica, and much of this century's) on the size and power of the phalluses which are active on every page. 'I was lost', writes Emily at one point,

> 'I was lost to everything but the wonderful instrument that was
> sheathed within me. I call it wonderful, and I think not improperly;
> for wonderful must that thing be that in the midst of the most poignant
> grief can so rapidly dissolve our senses with the softest sensations,
> spite of inclination, so quickly cause us to forget our early impressions,
> our first affections, and in the most forlorn and wretched moment of
> our existence make us taste such voluptuous delight and lustful
> pleasure. . . You, Silvia, who are yet I believe an inexperienced maid,
> can have no conception of the seductive powers of this wonderful
> instrument of nature – this terror of virgins but delight of women.'

Passages like these, however comic they may seem in their posturings, and however patently male in the reflections of their female characters, at least make this book more readable, more amusing, providing breathing-space between orgies, as it were. The anonymous author clearly thought of his book as more, if only a little more, than a simple work of pornography.

Dolly Morton

This is certainly also true of *The memoirs of Dolly Morton. The Story of a woman's part in the struggle to free the slaves. An account of the whippings, rapes and violences that preceded the Civil War in America. With curious anthropological observations on the radical diversities in the conformation of the Female Bottom and the way different women endure Chastisement.*

Clearly, we are back in the flagellation fields. But that apart, *Dolly Morton*, which appeared in 1899, is a cut above the usual Victorian erotic novel. It was published by one Charles Carrington and was written in French (entitled *En Virginie*) by a friend of his, Hugues Rebell (who called himself 'Georges Grassal'). It was quickly translated and a preface was added which paid tribute to the brave women who fought to free the slaves. In the course of her work for this noble cause, Miss Morton was thoroughly whipped on a regular basis: Rebell was clearly one of those men who believed that, in the words of the author of *Raped on the Railway*, 'there is nothing makes a woman so randy as a good flogging, and nothing so much excites a man as flogging a woman or seeing her flogged.'

Those readers who do not share this view will find many pages of *Dolly Morton* extremely boring; the theme is, so to say, flogged to death, and at every level from mere spanking to near-murder. However, there is no denying that the book, inter alia, gives a striking and powerful account of life in the South before the Civil War; the author was clearly a student of American history – and the setting has the advantage, unlike the fake-Eastern fripperies of the Harem books, of making his story atmospherically believable.

Rebell later wrote a second flagellation story, *Frank and I* (1902), in which Frank, a runaway schoolboy, is captured by the narrator, and found to be a girl who discovers as much pleasure in being whipped as the narrator has in whipping her (all these books have in common the fact that their heroines, at first horrified at the mere sight of the whip, eventually find that its use gives them the utmost pleasure).

Flagellation remains a moderately popular theme in twentieth century English erotic books – many contain at least one flagellation scene (some publishers encourage this – see p.72) though it is now extremely unusual to find one which consists of almost nothing but flogging – as did so many Victorian novels: *Lady Bumtickler's Revels, With Rod and Bum*, or *Sport in the West-End of London*, and (a title extensive even by Victorian standards) *The Experimental Lecture of Colonel Spanker on the Exciting and Voluptuous Pleasures to be derived from crushing and humiliating the spirit of a beautiful and modest young lady, as delivered to him in the Assembly Room of the Society of Aristocratic Flagellants, Mayfair* (which the aficionado Henry Spencer Ashbee described as 'the most coldly cruel and unblushingly indecent of any [book] we have ever read').

The reference to 'crushing and humiliating the spirit' of a heroine is significant, for the subjugation of women is a constant theme not only in the *Moorish Harem* but in most Victorian erotica. This was not wilful – the writers were simply reflecting the climate of the time. After all, the women in *Middlemarch* and *Jane Eyre* are scarcely models of assertion. The powerful women in Dickens are not his heroines, but certain minor characters – he equates passion on the whole with violence, the examples including not only Bill Sikes and Nancy, but Quilp in *The Old Curiosity Shop*. In none of his novels is there any scene which suggests that his characters think of sex as a delightful pleasure.

Turn to the nineteenth century erotic novelist and one finds much the same view expressed: all right, sex is a pleasure, and no mistake about it – but a pleasure to be taken by the man at the expense of the woman, who if she is not struggling in an exciting fashion against the male aggressor, simply lies back and thinks of England – occasionally however admiring her lover for his stamina and the size of his phallus. In *Raped on the Railway*, which came out in 1894, and was one of the most popular pieces of pornography of its time, the heroine, violently attacked by the hero in a non-corridor train, is at first repelled by him – but on his explaining that he only raped her because he found her beauty irresistible, 'woman-like burst into a flood of tears' and forgave him. (Later, admittedly, she managed to dislocate the penis of another attacker – a nice trick if you can do it, and one which in this case proves fatal).

Frequent gay scenes

One of the interesting things about Victorian erotica is the regular appearance of gay scenes – at a time when (as poor Oscar Wilde was to learn) any physical expression of homosexuality was illegal. Lesbian scenes were of course common: less surprising, for the law did not prohibit such activity (allegedly because Queen Victoria could not believe that it could possibly take place). Many brothels provided lesbian *tableaux* as a form of extra stimulation for their customers. Gay brothels for men did of course exist, including the one at 19, Cleveland Street frequented by the heir to the throne, the dissolute Prince Albert Victor ('Eddy'); they but were regarded as even more degenerate than heterosexual brothels. However, the 'given' view of the Victorian male as perhaps sentimental but wholly and blatantly masculine takes a severe knock when one looks at the erotic books he enjoyed.

One of the most popular early Victorian gay texts resembles the columns devoted in the twentieth century tabloid press to sexual scandals of various sorts, printed only, of course, to make public evidence of indecent behaviour by public figures, and not with the faintest idea of titillation. In 1813, an anonymous publisher brought out *The Phoenix of Sodom, or the Vere Street Coterie* – a vivid description of the goings on at the Swan, a pub in Vere Street, London, which had been raided by the police three years earlier.

Two soldiers found in compromising circumstances there were actually executed, and seven other men imprisoned. The behaviour for which they were condemned was described in great detail, as were the men themselves – including a coal merchant who called himself Kitty Cambric and a drummer boy known as Black-eyed Leonora.

Two books followed the Cleveland Street scandal of 1871: one, *The Sins of the Cities of the Plain*, is an account of a Victorian rent boy, and though clearly much of it is invention, a great deal rings true. Such books have their uses, and their publishers gain from two kinds of sales: to people genuinely interested in sociology and to those simply interested in sex. There are many twentieth century examples, from accounts of the Profumo scandal on.

Erotic correspondence

To turn to non-fiction, apart from Walter, Restif, Casanova and the rest, very few genuinely erotic love letters have found their way into print. This is not perhaps surprising as a love letter is written to the recipient alone, and it would be a kind of betrayal even to think of publication. The receiver, too, is far more likely to dispose of such letters in some way than to keep them safe for some future publisher. James Joyce's letters to his wife are an exception, though only readers who share his scatological tastes will find them erotic. Another remarkable exception is a series of letters written by the eccentric Fr Rolfe, 'Baron Corvo', to a Quaker friend who shared his homosexual tastes, and whom he titillated with his description of his adventures with the Venetian boys he loved. The critic Pamela Hansford Johnson wrote of these letters that there was 'something splendid, almost mythological, about their ramping sexuality; it was so extremely wholehearted. . .' It is difficult not to agree with her: picking up a young dock worker, Fr Rolfe took him to a wineshop, where they carried their glasses to the back of the shop and the boy told Rolfe about his life. Seeing his companion no doubt as a possible patron,

> ' "First, Sior, see my person", he said. And the vivacious creature did all which follows in about 30 seconds of time. Not more. I have said that we were sitting side by side at the little table. Moving, every inch of him, as swiftly and smoothly as a cat, he stood up, casting a quick glance into the shop to make sure that no one noticed. Only the sleepy proprietor slept there. He rolled his coat into a pillow and put it on my end of the table, ripped open his trousers, stripped them down to his feet, and sat bare bottomed on the other end. He turned his shirt right up over his head holding it in one hand, opened his arms wide and lay

back along the little table with his shoulders on the pillow (so that his breast and belly and thighs formed one slightly slanting line, unbroken by the arch of the ribs, as is the case with flat distention) and his beautiful throat and his rosy, laughing face strained backward while his widely open arms were an invitation. He was just one brilliant rosy series of muscles, smooth as satin, breasts and belly and groin and closely folded thighs with (in the midst of the black blossom of exuberant robustitude) a yard like a rose-tipped lance. And – the fragrance of his healthy youth and of the lily-flowers' dust was intoxicating. He crossed his ankles, ground his thighs together with a gently rippling motion, writhed his groin and hips once or twice and stiffened into the most inviting mass of fresh meat conceivable, laughing in my face as he made his offering of lively flesh. And the next instant he was up, his trousers buttoned, his shirt tucked in and his cloak folded around him.'

While in the 1990s we are not especially happy to have anyone – even a Venetian rent boy – described as an 'inviting mass of fresh meat', the situation itself is undeniably conveyed with a woderfully vivacious pen. Compare it with Fanny Hill's description of her lover on p.30; if this is what you want to write, this is the way to write it.

It is interesting to speculate whether any of the writers from whom I have quoted so far would have written any differently had the law allowed them to publish freely. The answer is probably that they would not – though one or two of them might have enriched their published works by enlarging them to contain some passages they had to publish clandestinely. In our own time the law may have changed, but the quality – sometimes, of course the lack of quality – has remained much the same.

4
Modern
erotic fiction

One of the results of the loosening of the censorship laws and the general change in the climate of public opinion, where the publication of erotic literature are concerned, is that writers who are generally highly regarded as poets, playwrights and novelists, have not hesitated to publish work which is direct and forthright in sexual expression.

Joe Orton

As contemporary diaries go, though the journals of Denton Welch contain scenes of considerable homoerotic sensitivity, beautifully written, and Anaïs Nin's journals have some predictably fine passages, the most striking recent example of eroticism conveyed to startling effect is in the diaries of the playwright Joe Orton (1933-1967). It was Orton's agent who suggested he might keep a diary, probably for publication – and it seems to be an accurate record of his outrageous life, though it could certainly not have been published in the 1960s. His writing has an urgency which suggests that he described each event soon after it happened (the sentences are short, breathless), and some people will perhaps find passages as 'offensive' as some passages in 'Walter' or Harris. Even though Orton was capable of a quick pick-up in a 'cottage', and recorded such events without sentimentality, his journal is not entirely devoid of tenderness, and on the whole doesn't leave too unpleasant a taste. (If tenderness in the kind of situation he describes seems impossible, it is worth remembering that one of the most beautiful love poems of the twentieth century, W. H. Auden's 'Lay your sleeping head, my love', was written to a German rent boy.)

It seems obvious that Orton was writing for posterity. Many diarists are, of course; and our loss is the freedom and unself-consciousness which, while maybe inelegant and unstylish, is vivid and blood-hot. But Orton was right in carefully crafting his erotic scenes (if that is what he did), for lust does not necessarily

convey itself best, on the page, when written at blood heat, as
we see in Walter's autobiography. Here is one passage which
seems to work well both as believable record and as a piece of
erotic prose:

> '[The Tunisian boy] was standing under a tree in the rain. He smiled,
> I nodded in the direction of the waste ground opposite the beach.
> He took my hand and we ran across the wasteland in the rain. We
> reached the flat and I had difficulty in finding how to open it.
> Fortunately nobody came up. . . The boy stood in the centre of the
> room. I tried to explain that this apartment belonged to a friend. He
> seemed to understand neither French, English or Spanish. I took him
> to the bed. Kissed him. He was shy and didn't open his mouth. He
> got very excited then I undressed him. I undressed myself and we
> lay caressing each other for about ten minutes. He had a loutish
> body, large cock, but not so large as to make me envious or shy. I
> turned him over. He wouldn't let me get in so I fucked along the line
> of his buttocks which was very exciting. He'd wiped his spit on his
> bum. When I'd come a great patch on Bill Fox's coverlet, I went and
> fetched a towel – then we kissed some more, neck, cheeks, eyes. . .
> He then turned me over and came along the line of my buttocks in
> the same way. Suddenly he stopped and said, 'How much you give
> me?' 'Five dirham,' I said. 'No, please, fifteen.' 'No,' I said, 'five.'
> He grinned. 'OK,' he said, and went on. He took a very long time to
> come. We lay together for an hour afterwards while the rain poured
> down outside and the thunder roared. His name is Mohammed. We
> then took a shower together. I then gave him five dirhams, slipped it
> into his pocket. He said, 'Please, one more.' Because he was sweet,
> and even on a matter of one dirham they like to gain a victory, I
> gave him an extra. He kissed my cheek, I hugged him and said
> I'd see him again.'

The idea that such a passage might ever make its way into print
would have seemed ridiculous not too long ago. As ridiculous as
it would have seemed to the Victorians that a complete edition
of Pepys' diary would ever be published (though it might be
noted in passing that the editors of that marvellous publishing
accomplishment have left all the more intimate passages in the
largely invented language in which Pepys described them).

But in the 1990s, anything goes – the way cleared by the epoch-
making *Lady Chatterley* case, novels sprang into print in the 1970s
which would have been unpublishable previously. The few legal
cases since then have underlined the fact that while the law may
consider certain publications illegal, juries are not on the whole
prepared to condemn books which while they may certainly not be
much to do with 'literature', are produced merely to give their
readers a sexual thrill.

'Serious' novels have profited from this change in the wind, of course; and though certain great novelists seem incapable of writing passionately or credibly about sex (Graham Greene and Evelyn Waugh are only two examples) other fine writers have taken advantage of the new climate.

Lolita

A prime example is Vladimir Nobokov's *Lolita* – the story of a middle-aged man's passion for a 'nymphet', a girl of between nine and fourteen, which was banned for a while, but later published, with enormous sales. Nabokov clearly wanted, perhaps needed, to write the novel. Even today, paedophilia is so strong a taboo that were the novel not written by a 'respectable' author in rather 'difficult' prose, and with only a limited number of overtly sexual scenes, it would perhaps be unlikely to find a publisher. *Lolita* manages to avoid depravity by various means: above all by humour, but also by the eponymous heroine's complete disregard for her lover's sexual feelings. 'My life [the narrator's penis] was handled by little Lo in an energetic, matter-of-fact manner as if it were an insensate gadget unconnected with me.' Lolita's instinctive knowingness does not count where a censor is concerned: such niceties are on the whole uncommon among those who criticise overt sexuality; so is irony.

But books or passages in books depicting sex involving children beneath the age of consent are resisted by most publishers, even when the writers concerned have extremely reputable and well-known names. The opening pages of Nadine Gordimer's 1974 novel *The Conservationist* is one exception: in them, the narrator sits by the side of a young girl on a 'plane journey – a girl who 'looks no more than sixteen or seventeen' – and in an extremely erotic passage lifts her skirt, beneath the rug that covers their laps, and places his finger inside her.

For such a passage to be permissable in a 'serious' novel (how ridiculous the term is: does it mean there is no such thing as a serious erotic novel? – but on the other hand, how does one avoid it?) the writer must be very skilful indeed; but reading the text it is impossible to suppose that Ms Gordimer meant it *only* to arouse sexual feelings in her reader – though it is inevitable that it should do so.

Erotica for women

Women have entered the field with some enthusiasm. There is of course no reason why not. Anaïs Nin wrote in the Preface to *Delta of Venus* about the circumstances in which she began to write erotica:

> 'At the time we were all writing erotica at a dollar a page, I realised
> that for centuries we had had only one model for this literary genre
> – the writing of men. I was already conscious of a difference between
> the masculine and feminine treatment of sexual experience. I knew
> that there was a great disparity between Henry Miller's explicitness
> and my ambiguities – between his humorous, Rabelaisian view of
> sex and my poetic descriptions of sexual relationships. . . women, I
> thought, were more apt to fuse sex with emotion, with love, and to
> single out one man rather than be promiscuous. . . but although
> women's attitude towards sex was quite distinct from that of men,
> we had not yet learned how to write about it. . .
>   [Re-reading her erotica] 'In numerous passages I was intuitively
> using a woman's language, seeing sexual experience from a woman's
> point of view. I finally decided to release the erotica for publication
> [in 1969] because it shows the beginning efforts of a woman in a world
> that had been the domain of men.'

In the 1990s, the British publishing firm Virgin decided to start an
imprint which would issue erotic books specifically written for
women. Many people predicted disaster: there was little evidence to
show that women were interested in erotica. *Playboy*, a magazine
featuring soft-porn photographs of men and text similar to that in
its counterpart, *Playgirl* – more or less pornographic essays and
short stories, and 'confessional' letters from readers – had been
bought chiefly by gay men; sexologists claimed that surveys
showed women were uninterested in reading about sex. However,
within a year Black Lace books were selling steadily, and some of
them – Portia da Costa's *Gemini Heat* and Frederica Alleyn's
Cassandra's Conflict – had gone into six or seven reprints, with sales
of something over 30,000 copies each. By 1994 the total sales were
over 400,000 copies, and two new titles were being published each
month. Interestingly, the publishers printed a questionnaire at the
back of each novel and from a very large number of replies were
able to build up a picture of their readers, who were indeed
predominantly women: only 27 per cent of the books were bought
by men (and not particularly by gay men). Some of the comments
from readers were illuminating: a nursery nurse in her thirties cried
'At long last – getting away from Cartland virgins!', while an
administrative supervisor confirmed that it was 'about time we had
books like this for women.' These were books 'for sexually aware
women, and not brain dead bimbos', and a teacher in her thirties felt
it was 'good to know I'm not abnormal in wanting to read erotica.'
The readers of these books are, it is claimed, educated women, fifty
per cent of them from social groups A, B and C1, and with an

income above the average (between £10,000 and £30,000 a year). Several mentioned their delight that erotica could be bought at W. H. Smith's (a company notably hesitant to stock male erotica).

A considerable number of them claimed that their sex lives improved as a result of reading the books (usually with their partners, in bed). What this suggests is that they felt exactly as many men feel, and enjoyed reading Black Lace books for much the same reasons that men enjoyed reading Nexus books (Virgin's male orientated list): they wanted some fantasy, they wanted to read about sexual variety even if they could not actually enjoy it.

They also made it quite clear what they wanted to find between the books' covers: this included an adventurous and independent heroine and a sexually dominant, rugged, charming, hunky and romantic hero. The couple would ideally enjoy themselves in some exotic setting – jungles and desert islands were among the top choices, with deserts and Middle East harems not far behind (few readers were interested in castles or dungeons); a quarter of the readers preferred the books to be set in the present day, but quite a number enjoyed almost any period from medieval and barbarian to sci-fi settings.

'Anything goes'?

As to the sex itself, preferences were almost evenly spread: readers looked forward to submissive females, group sex, flagellation, bondage and fetishism, 'experimental sex' – only ten per cent enjoying stories involving lesbianism and five per cent requesting some gay male sex. Black Lace's survey certainly deals a blow to any suggestion that quite a large number of women are not as interested as men in overt sexuality on the page; and for most of them 'anything goes' – in books, at least; there is no suggestion that their involvement goes beyond fantasy, or that they have any desire to experience in real life what they experience vicariously in books.

'Serious' women novelists have, post-Nin, also written about sex with increasing frankness. The first two notable books by women authors which were more overtly and exclusively sexual than any of recent years, came from French writers – Benoîte Groult's *Salt on our Skin*, described as 'a passionate dissection of physical lust', and Alina Reyes' *The Butcher*, both of which were wildly successful. Whether the Black Lace authors (or publishers) saw the success and decided to follow it is doubtful: perhaps the stronger sexual meat of recent women's fiction was a simple progression from such books as *Hollywood Wives* and *Lace*, in which Jackie Collins and Shirley

Conran wrote franker sex scenes than most other women writers had previously done.

Collins and Conran need no excuses, surely, any more than the Black Lace publishers: but there is evidence which they could have produced to excuse their more open approach to sexuality. Linda Grant (*Sexing the Millenium*) and other writers on the subject claim that both writing and reading about sex is actually good for women:

> 'It's liberating and empowering, and enables women to get in touch with how they really feel sexually, instead of internalising the objectified images of themselves that they get from films made by men.'

Certainly if one looks at the best-selling novels of the past twenty years, it is the women who have written the most successful sex scenes: Jeffrey Archer, Frederick Forsyth, are left far behind (admittedly sex plays a very small part indeed in their books). The surprise and even shock felt by some (mostly male) journalists at the fact that women can, or want to, write sex scenes has resulted in some rather strange classifications. Reading her books, one wonders how Jilly Cooper has become known as *the* British woman writer of 'sexy books'. Her descriptions of allegedly sexy men and women are often too obvious to be effective, and her sense of humour keeps getting in the way of the action. For instance, in *Polo* (1991) the 'airplane billionaire' Bart Alderton is flying the all too willing Chessie over the English countryside in a helicopter:

> ' "Take your dress off," said Bart idly. "Just undo the harness and take it off."
> ' "Ker-ist," he said a moment later, as Chessie threw the dress behind her seat. "Oh, Christ."
> 'She was only wearing a pair of rose-patterned white pants. The slenderness of her waist emphasised the fullness of her thighs, and her breasts soft and white-gold in the sunshine with the nipples pink and spread. Her cheeks were very flushed, her eyelids drooped over eyes leaden with lust. . .
> ' "Two joy-sticks," murmured Chessie, putting her hand on his cock. "I know which one I'd like best." '

And later, in the middle of a torrid love scene, when the polo-playing Angel Solis de Gonzales is busily engaged with Bart's daughter Bibi, the author punctures the atmosphere with

> '[he] slid two fingers between her legs. Christ, he could restore polo sticks in the slippery linseed oiliness.'

Good fun; but erotic?

Again, Jackie Collins' reputation for 'raunchiness' (perhaps something different, incidentally, from eroticism?) is questionable when one actually reads her books. In her best-selling *Hollywood Wives* (1983) the sex scenes are actually very cooly and almost clinically described:

> 'She tended both Gina and Neil at once, touching first Gina's ripe nipples, then Neil's rampant penis which threatened to burst, the skin was stretched so tight.
>
> 'She fussed and fretted over each of them, her long hair trailing on their skin like strands of fine silken thread.
>
> 'After a while it was torture.
>
> 'Exquisite torture.
>
> 'He shoved the Eurasian girl away and mounted Gina, who wanted him as much as he wanted her. She was so wet and ready that he almost slipped out, but Thiou-Ling had not deserted them, she was there to help him enter the moist warmth of the second most popular blonde in America. She guided him into paradise . . .'

Shirley Conran, the doyenne of sex'n'shopping, is a writer of another kind. It may be that a lifetime spent working with words has been a help (she was for many years a distinguished journalist and magazine feature writer before turning to fiction); but her sex scenes are written with real skill as well as panache and originality, the situations often ingenious and surprising, and vividly described. In *Lace* (1982), for instance, two of her characters, Maxine and Charles, are being shown around his champagne *caves*, and he insists on making love to her, dangerously, under the eyes of his employees. Though there is relatively little overt sexual language, the sensual voltage is remarkably high. Not that Ms Conran is in the least mealy-mouthed: there are several scenes, later in the book, between Judy, one of the book's four heroines, and Griffin, a publisher, in which no holds are barred, and in which the description is extremely graphic – but where again there is considerable sensitivity to atmosphere. The author knows how to match action with just the right tone of voice.

When more conventional, 'serious' novelists turn to sex, a satisfactorily high voltage can be difficult for them to attain. Maureen Freely, whose novel *Under the Vulcania* (1984) is about nothing but sex, certainly found this to be true: 'I wanted to banish the judge in my imagination, Madame Bluestocking, who was always keeping tabs on me. I did it to please myself,' she has said. And it did, as it pleased many readers – and even some critics. Her book is about a highly professional brothel for women, established somewhere in England (there are references which suggest the, on the face of it, unlikely venue of Bath, Ms Freely's home city). She has not the enthusiasm for minute description that the Misses da Costa and Alleyn enjoy, but the heated atmosphere is well done, and the psychological implications of the characters' tastes and actions are more thoroughly explored than in most erotic fiction.

Although the editors of erotica for women claim that they can tell instantly whether a manuscript has been written by a woman or a man, I beg leave to doubt it. Certainly on the basis of published books, there seems to be little difference between male and female erotic fantasies. Interestingly, the editors of the Black Lace list suggest that many more women would read erotica ostensibly published for men, if the covers were not so chauvinistic: it would be interesting if some publishers of exclusively male erotica were to think about this. It may of course be the case that ostentatiously masculine men would hesitate to buy books without an adequate show of naked female breasts and buttocks on the cover, and that gaining a large number of woman readers publisher might lose a larger number of male ones.

Male erotic fiction has been, until the past year or so, more readily available than female – and it is unlikely that anyone who has sufficient interest in the subject to pick up this book has not explored it to some extent. Certainly, anyone intending to write for this market should lay their hands on a considerable selection and do their own market analysis; but in addition, besides the 'classic' erotic texts (which certainly embrace some Victorian erotica) there is much to be learned from general reading of first-rate twentieth century authors whose writing about sexuality is skilful and enjoyable: the bibliography at the end of this book makes some suggestions.

5
Practical
matters

The history of the erotic novel has a great deal to teach us about various possible approaches to the subject; and the extracts which I have quoted so far and quote in Chapter 6 should be helpful in demonstrating the various ways in which the writer can approach sex scenes (I cannot too strongly recommend reading the complete works, however – see the Bibliography on p.107; but see also the shelves of your local bookshop for the most recent erotic books).

Let's now turn to practical matters.

I assume that we are talking about good erotic writing rather than what I have vaguely called pornographic or obscene. Though erotic books which claim to be nothing else are often sneered at, some are written to rather a high standard. I assume that there is very little point in striving to write a bad erotic book – though provided the sex is sufficiently heated, some bad erotic books (like the worst Victorian pornography) have been commercially extremely successful. Let's forget that, however, and suppose that we want to write an erotic book which is successful not only in that it sells, but that it is good of its kind – with at least some believable and likable characters, and a plot which is at least sufficiently robust to carry them on to the end of the book.

The naming of parts

Plot, characters, motivation – all the things which are important in writing a conventional novel – are important in writing erotic novels, but the problem of language in erotic literature is, at the time of writing, particularly difficult – much more difficult, probably, than for earlier generations.

One reason for this is that certain words which once held a strong erotic charge have become thoroughly familiar as common swear words. Until the 1960s, the shock of seeing such a word as 'cock' in cold print was enough to give at least a diminutive sexual *frisson*; these days, language has almost lost the power to shock of its own volition. Anyone over the age of fifty or so may well remember the first time they saw 'rude words' in print (these were the days when the picture editors of *Health and Efficiency* still air-brushed out the pubic hair of any woman facing the camera, while men always tactfully faced away from the lens). The very presence even of a single 'cock' argued that one was reading what one shouldn't – in 'respectable' books the convention was still to write 'f---' and 'c---'. Looking into one of those spectacularly naughty green-covered paperbacks which were published in the famous *Travellers' Library* list which one smuggled back from Paris in the 1950s, one was conscious of a store of depravity previously unsampled.

Even now, reading books of an earlier generation, the appearance of a particular – not always overtly sexual – word can still give one some idea of the shock which it must originally have given its first readers. Take Thomas Hardy's *The Woodlanders*, for instance: in chapter thirty-three the book's heroine, Grace Melbury, and Mrs Charmond, the woman with whom her husband has been having an affair, get lost in the woods and huddle together for warmth. In the intimacy which results, Mrs Charmond confesses all, and in an extraordinary moment: '"O, my great God!" [Grace] exclaimed, thunderstruck at a revelation transcending her utmost suspicion, "He's had you!"' The frank expression, so completely unexpected, strikes home, in context, with an astonishing effect. It is an object lesson, even now, in how to achieve an effect of sexual shock without using language which could be in any way offensive to anyone: brought about by Hardy's success in depicting a girl so sweet and innocent that the words she speaks are as startling, from her lips, as the strongest language from another's.

We are not entirely past the time when we can make such an effect; but it is not easy when the commonest sexual language is heard every day in the playground. It is a very great advantage lost.

Innocent language

As in so many other areas of erotic prose, the most extraordinary example of innocence of language is to be found in *Fanny Hill*: there is not a word in Cleland's novel which would bring a blush to the cheek of the most virginal reader. The situations are as lecherous as may be, but they are described in prose which might be that of a sermon. Take, for instance, Fanny's first view of a penis – belonging to a gentleman entertained by the madam of a brothel into which our heroine has been recruited:

'Her sturdy stallion had now unbutton'd, and produced naked, stiff, and erect, that wonderful machine, which I had never seen before, and which, for the interest my own seat of pleasure began to take furiously in it, I star'd at with all the eyes I had. . .'

And a few pages later, a second customer appears, entertained by a colleague:

'Then his grand movement, which seem'd to rise out of a thicket of curling hair that spread from the root all round thighs and belly up to the navel, stood stiff and upright, but of a size to frighten me, by sympathy, for the small tender part which was the object of its fury. . .'

Contrast with the description of a somewhat similar scene in a 1990s novel:

'His cock was purple and stiff, standing up against his belly so that she could see his enormous balls, now no longer swinging but drawn up between his thighs, the hair which covered them lank and shining with sweat. So this was what she had been waiting for. It was an enormous prick – bigger than she had thought possible. But she opened the lips of her cunt to him, and. . .'

Well, there is no need to go on. It is not that the circumstances are any different, or indeed the actions which arise out of them; it is just that the obvious nouns are so obvious, so unsurprising, so unshocking and so lacking in even the faintest nuance.

The elegance of Cleland's prose was a product of his own genius; but though other writers of his time and earlier used coarser language – as a glance at Rochester reveals – there is not a word in Fanny Hill to frighten a child. A much earlier author, Jean de Meun (c.1250-c.1305), who wrote part of the famous *Romance of the Rose*, also declined to use 'rough language' (as he called it) but relied instead on metaphor and allegory:

'[Nature] gave me the rod herself, and wanted it polished before I learned to read. There was no need whatever to tip it: it was serviceable without. Ever since she gave it to me, I've kept it safe, kept it always to hand. I'll do my best never to lose it, for I value it more than a million gold pieces. It delights me to look at it, and when I feel it fulfilled and happy, I thank her with all my heart. How often it's comforted me in my travels!. . .

'My intention, if I could haul my tackle to a harbour, was to bring it close enough to the holy objects to touch them. I'd been through so much and come so far, untipped rod or no! I knelt, eagerly, zestfully, between the two lovely pillars, consumed with eagerness to worship the beautiful, sacred sanctuary with a devoted and pious heart. . .
I moved aside the curtain which covered the holy objects, and moved to explore the sacred place more intimately. I kissed the holy spot devotedly, and then tried to put my rod into the aperture, with the sack hanging behind. . .'

And so on.

The Chinese of the early Confucian age used equally ingenious and much more poetic simile and metaphor. They deeply disapproved of chastity and reverenced sex as life-enhancing in every way. Jade, the most valuable element in nature, was believed to be the fossilised semen of the Celestial Dragon, so making love one drank at the fountain of jade; the penis was a fountain of jade upon which a woman could play with fingers and lips, while a man strove to enter the gateway of jade. The penis was also sometimes called a stallion or a tree, the vagina a deer, a peach, a lemon; clouds, wind, rain were all metaphors for making love – and all these images appear in Chinese painting as well as literature. Such novels as *Chin P'ing Mei*, or *The Golden Lotus* (c.1595) and *Jou Pu Tuan* or *The Before Midnight Scholar* (written by Li Yu in the seventeenth century) are well worth reading for their beauty of imagery, and as examples similar to *Fanny Hill* in their avoidance of coarseness.

Victorian writers of pornography felt under no compulsion to be artists. Turn to *The Pearl*, published a little over a century later, and the vocabulary is very different to that of Cleland. Open any page at random and one finds what used coyly to be called 'Anglo-Saxon words' everywhere. But at least the Victorians had, though they did not always make use of it – one advantage not open to us: a wonderful field of inventive sexual slang.

The uses of slang

A splendid anthology of these is to be found in the remarkable *Dictionary of the Vulgar Tongue* published in 1811, derived by a Captain Grose, with the help of 'Hell-Fire Dick and James Gordon, Esqrs, of Cambridge, and William Soames, Esq. of the Hon. Society of Newman's Hotel', from an earlier dictionary which had come out in 1785. There is a lot of thieves' slang in the dictionary, and some fascinating revelations (such as the use of the word 'pigs' for policemen almost two hundred years ago); but the treasure trove for writers of erotica is the lovers' or philanderers' slang. There is too much of this to quote extensively (the *Dictionary* really is essential reading) – but here are a few examples:

> *Abbess* – the mistress of a brothel; *bob tail* – a lewd woman; *buttered bun* – one lying with a woman that has just laid with another man is said to have a buttered bun; *crinkum crankum* – 'a woman's commodity'; *double jugg* – a man's back side; *gaying instrument* – the penis; *to grind* – to have carnal knowledge of a woman; *to jock* – to enjoy a woman; *lobcock* – a large, relaxed penis; *plug tail* – a penis; *sugar stick* – the virile member

and so on. If you are inventive enough, you can of course devise your own slang terms: François Rabelais (c.1494-c.1553) was, unsurprisingly, wonderfully good at this – Gargantua's nurses and governesses (and mistresses) poured out a veritable cornucopia of euphemisms for his penis:

> 'One of them would call it her pillicock, her fiddle-diddle, her staff of love, her tickle-gizzard, her gentle titler. Another, her sugar-plum, her kingo, her old rowley, her touch-trap, her flap dowdle. Another again, her branch of coral, her placket-racket, her Cyprian sceptre, her tit-bit, her bob-lady. And some of the other women would give these names, my Roger, my cockatoo, my nimble-wimble, bush-beater, claw-buttock, eves-fropper, pick-lock, pioneer, bully-ruffin, smell-smock, trouble-gusset, my lusty live sausage, my crimson chitterlin, rump-splitter, shove-devil, down right to it, sniff and snout, in and to, at her again, my coney-burrow-ferret, wily-beguiley, my pretty rogue. . .

We seem largely to have lost this kind of inventive talent – though Francis King, in his entertaining pastische *Danny Hill* (Danny, of course, being the sister of the better-known Fanny) invented the expression 'riding-muscle' for penis, which works so well that it is difficult not to believe that he did not find it in some little-known eighteenth century novel.

Sometimes, the right term suggests itself because of the character or period one is writing about: Falstaff, the eponymous hero of Robert Nye's fictional autobiography, speaks of his 'sword' – as the character himself might well have done. Nye and Anthony Burgess (in his novel on Shakespeare's life, *Nothing like the Sun*), prove themselves masters of slang and bawdy – as of course was Shakespeare himself – see Eric Partridge's *Shakespeare's Bawdy*, first published in a limited edition of 1,000 (so naughty was it) in 1947. Happily, though reprinted many times, this book has clearly never been seen by any recent Minister of Education, or the study of Shakespeare would surely have been banned from our schools.

Partridge's great *Dictionary of Slang and Unconventional English* enshrines an even greater hoard, and no serious writer of erotica should be without it. Open it at random: on almost every page there is a word which can be used in the right context: *fancy Joseph* – a harlot's lover or ponce; *knock* - to have sexual intercourse with; *peel* - to undress; *to shoot the milt* – to ejaculate. It is possible to use many of these terms even in a contemporary setting – a number of them indeed are still in use.

Our equivalent modern slang is of course often just as vigorous, and often just as picturesque: innumerable terms for intercourse – ball, bang, do, frig, charver; for parts of the body – bald-headed hermit, blow stick, Irish root, middle leg, pork sword, tummy banana; or beaver, cranny, furry hoop, golden doughnut, muffin, pussy. . .

The problem is that while these may be used (usually in dialogue, and provided they are in character) in the course of a serious novel in which there are one or two sex scenes, it is difficult to use them in a book which is primarily a series of copulations. They sound, basically, comic; the slang of previous centuries has a veneer of romance which gives them the sort of period flavour which contributes something to an erotic scene rather than detracting by humour. Humour is a great dampener of the erotic impulse: more of that, later.

Boring repetition

But surely, you might say, the language doesn't matter all that much? – readers don't go to erotica for fine language? Of course not. But such research as has been done on the subject indicates that most readers of erotica – those, that is, who are readers in the sense that they read all sorts of books – tend to dislike what for want of a better word one must I suppose call 'coarseness', if not in the situations, then in the language which describes them. And in any case, continual repetition of the ubiquitous *cock* and *cunt* and *fuck* are not only crass but extremely boring. *Cunt* and *fuck* in fact both present something of a problem: they are words now much associated with unthinking profanity and violence, and in the former case with extreme male chauvinism. In their advice to authors, the editors of the Black Lace erotic books written by women for women suggest that 'we would like the vocabulary to be less "blokey", using the word *fuck* only in speech, and avoiding the word *cunt* altogether.'

While it is true that 'fuck' is used so frequently and with so little sense that the word has virtually become meaningless, and must now be employed sparingly, it is difficult to avoid it altogether. Happily, there are slang equivalents which can be used in certain contexts – and will be effective, especially when certain characters are concerned: an Australian might talk of having a horry, an American black of a hot fling or a whip shack, a Spaniard of a chingazo, a Jew of a schtup. But in a contemporary setting the problem of what Henry Reed in a poem memorably called 'The Naming of Parts' remains a problem, which is no doubt why so many erotic writers – male writers, at all events – choose to set their books in the past, and usually in the Victorian past (perhaps because this also offers the opportunity for a little costume sex: all those voluminous clothes to be stripped away).

Some women writers are more inventive as to setting and period than men – but often simply because of that inventiveness they run up against the language problem with a resounding slap. One,

Sophie Danson (or rather 'Sophie Danson', for almost invariably erotic prose is published under a pseudonym, and frequently with the pretence that the writer is either foreign or dead) sets an erotic novel in Arthurian Britain. Fine; but from almost the first page we have a reference to a 'vigorous penis', while soon we have a couple of girls 'fingering their clitorises'. I am not sure what ladies called their lovers' cocks in Arthurian Britain, but I doubt very much whether they called them penises.

Does it matter? I'm afraid it does.

Every writer must find his/her way around this problem. (Admittedly, later, Ms Danson uses 'pizzle' and 'prick', both of which, simply because they are unsophisticated slang terms, are perfectly acceptable, though just as anachronistic).

The instinctive ear

The problem is one which demands a certain amount of thought; the use of language in an erotic novel may not be crucial, but it is very important; bad or careless usage can distract the reader from, to coin a phrase, the matter in hand. As with all writing, what is necessary is a good ear – the instinct for what quite simply sounds wrong – you either have it or you haven't, though certainly it can be sharpened and honed in various ways – in particular, by reading.

As I have suggested, a good collection of slang dictionaries is a help – and since in most of them the sexual slang is buried amidst all the rest, it is quite a good idea to make your own, separate dictionary of sexual synonyms on disk.

Writing erotic prose is unlike most other kinds of writing in that there is a certain mechanical scenic repetitiveness about it: you must provide at least two sex scenes per chapter, or one every couple of thousand words or so, and it would certainly be a mistake to let much more than one thousand words of mere conventional narrative pass without either preparing for the next sex scene (by setting up some kind of sensuous location) or having something to say about the result (psychological or physiological) of the last one. This is rather like having to set up a dinner party scene every few pages – you had better have a good store of dishes in mind; however bright your imagination, you will need all the help you can get as far as language is concerned.

The plot

Some people claim that the plot is as nearly superfluous, in an erotic novel, as may be. But while it may be true that practically nobody picks up such a novel in order to be delighted by the twists and turns of the story, a plot is nevertheless necessary – and the evidence suggests that those erotic novels which are almost plotless are found less enjoyable, and certainly sell less well, than those which have enough plot to lead the reader credibly from one sexual episode to the another.

Story v. sex

The best (let's take that to mean the best-selling and most frequently reprinted) pornographic novels of the Victorian age were those with fairly strong plots and well-delineated characters (*Rape on the Railway* – see p.42 – is an obvious example). The story-telling instinct is a strong one, and seems to demand satisfaction even when we aren't, in principle, very much concerned with plot. Someone who picks up an erotic novel may believe that all he wants is a graphic description of continual sex; in fact, just that is very rarely what is wanted – the appetite soon cloys by what it feeds on. This is what makes anthologies of erotic fiction impossible to read straight through: to do so is like eating a meal consisting of seven courses of the same dish. A story involves the reader – even if the involvement in a plot is not as vital in the *genre* as it is for a thriller or a mystery.

What sort of plot does the erotic novel demand? Well, perhaps ironically in view of what I have just said, not a very strong one – and in fact not a very credible one: a story which is so involved that it distracts from the sex scenes is a bad idea. You should be looking forward, in an erotic novel, not to the next turn of the plot but the next turning down of the sheets. The sole purpose of the plot should be to provide a framework for a group of people who are going to perform a sexual charade: and the word *charade* is significant. You are, after all, writing a fantasy. Whatever critics of modern morals may suspect, the world in which people leap, every half hour and with undiminished enthusiasm, into each other's beds exists – happily or unhappily – only in erotic novels or stage farces. This makes your task both easier and more difficult: if 'anything goes' the devising of a plot and the people who inhabit it should not detain you long. But that idea is a trap: you have to maintain your balance between fantasy and credibility – your reader may know perfectly well that your book creates a mirage; knows perfectly well that such a string of events as you describe could never take place – yet he must find those events to some extent interesting.

So your story should *be* a story, and should have a beginning, middle and end; it can of course consist merely of a series of ten or fifteen separate adventures joined by the simplest narrative excuse (cf *The Decameron* or *Canterbury Tales*), though that format is rather prodigal of plot ideas. It is a good idea if possible to devise a plot in which sex already plays a part: a character bets another that he cannot bed a woman of every Zodiac sun-sign, from Aries to Pisces, or attempts to seduce the wife *and* two daughters of a judge. At all events the plot must offer sufficiently easy opportunities for sex to make the cavortings of your characters at least remotely believable. The setting ought also not to be too exacting: an erotic novel set inside the Arctic circle might be a little difficult to organise, simply because cold is not an aphrodisiac and an igloo not sufficiently spacious for more than the most confined orgy.

Classic erotic plots usually fall into relatively few categories. There are the romantic plots for instance which include those set in a Turkish Harem. The mysterious east may not be as mysterious as it once was, but set your novel sometime before 1900 and you have all the advantage of heat, desert sands, mysterious tents, diaphanous silken veils and handsome ruthless sheiks ('Why have you brought me here?' asks the innocent maiden of her seductive abductor. She will find out during the following 350 pages). These insatiable sheiks also possess, of course, a large harem, the equally ruthless, jealous (and frequently lesbian) members of which are naturally at once lascivious and possessed of insatiable sexual appetites. They provide more unusual experiences for the Ruined Maid.

The period plot

The period plot has the advantage not only of allowing the writer a more imaginative vocabulary but of making it easier to provide a ready supply of innocent young heroines whose virginity can be taken. These are not so readily available in the 1990s, at least not in fiction, and the theme has always been popular in erotic literature, when almost every virgin can be expected at the drop of a trouser immediately and conveniently to become a nymphomaniac. The clothes fetishist can have a great deal of fun writing about another age than his or her own, and the reader who shares the same tastes presumably has an equal amount of fun reading about it. One has an unfair vision of elderly gentlemen besotted with camisoles, knickers and long, silk stockings, though as research shows such readers are by no means necessarily elderly. Oddly, those who provide jackets for erotic novels seem fixated on the Victorian age, whatever the period of the novel they are illustrating. Pouting models in mock-Victorian underclothes are all over the bookshelves of service stations and airport terminals; whether readers are surprised when, opening the book, they find their 1880s maid actually living in 1820 – or 1920 for that matter – I can't say.

Just in order to allow yourself some fun by providing a problem or two, you can of course set yourself a conundrum: how is your hero to seduce the two daughters without the mother – or indeed the judge – catching on? But always remember that in making things difficult for yourself, you should not make them too difficult for the reader, who won't want to be kept too long from his or her fix of overt sex.

No reason why you shouldn't deal with real people, though some publishers say firmly that they don't favour the fictional biography or autobiography. There seems no real reason for this disapproval, however, provided the character you choose is one whose personality can support sensual fantasy. We may all have our own private reservations about this: there are some people of whose reputations we may be jealous. But should there be objection to a fictional life of Nell Gwynn or Harriet Wilson? Probably not – though you do set yourself the difficult task of making the account believable: your book could no longer be a complete fantasy, and those readers who picked it up would expect the period detail to be reasonably accurate. You would not only have this problem, which you could perhaps skate over fairly lightly; but you would have to make the chief protagonists reasonably believable as people, and in many cases (Miss Wilson's for instance) readers might compare your product to your character's autobiography, and the comparison might be odious.

The plot of an erotic novel must not, then, command too much attention from the reader: the simplest possible series of clashes between three or four characters can carry such a book forward quite satisfactorily, and can take place in any setting. The first lady of a harem threatened by the sudden arrival of a beautiful young virgin, who is fancied equally by the Dey and by his slave-master. . . Well, not a great deal of thought need be given to the subtleties of that situation.

On the other hand such a simple situation doesn't allow the writer to get much fun out of writing the book: yes, there is the setting – but once that is exhausted there is nowhere to go: you're stuck within its four walls. Choose to send your characters off to build the Great Western Railway and you can have fun researching the subject, while a whole line of possible settings immediately suggests itself – sex in a railway carriage, in a tunnel, in the ladies' waiting room; or whatever. Of course the setting is not all: you must provide an excuse for the characters to be involved – your hero might be engaged in buying the land for the railway (the seduction of various members of the landed gentry being necessary), or in guiding the necessary bill through Parliament (your heroine finding it imperative to persuade various Members to offer their support). And so on.

Any plot which would suit a conventional novel would do for an erotic novel, of course; but with the proviso that it must not be complicated, or rather you must not allow it to get complicated. For one thing, you won't have the space. In a novel of 80,000 words, you can probably only afford to devote at most 20,000 words to your plot: the rest will be devoted to providing the reader with what he or she wants of this particular book – sex.

The two of course are not mutually exclusive; in forwarding the plot there are all sorts of ways in which you can use erotic scenes – the flashback can be very useful, for instance, as can the device of having a minor character describe their own amorous adventures to your narrator.

Having fun

This is as good a place as any to say that it is absolutely vital to have fun, as a writer of erotic fiction. If you do not do so, the writing will be a miserable job, as grindingly boring a way of making a few pounds as could be thought of – and the resulting book will very likely indeed not be very good read. Fortunately, most writers of erotic fiction *do* enjoy writing it and would probably not have set out on their course in the first place if that had not been the case. They are people who enjoy sex and believe it to be one of the most joyful occupations provided for humanity by a benevolent creator, and are happy to convey that view to their readers. But since a certain amount of non-sexual narrative must appear in any book, it will be a good thing to devise a plot or a period which will keep you interested during the duller passages: a little research into gentleman's underclothing during the seventeenth century, or into women's perfume or make-up in Victorian England; or into Georgian Bath, or Regency Brighton, will help to lighten the task.

A story set sometime before, say, 1930, means that there can be interplay between servants and the Upper Classes; and it is of course a known fact that footmen are immeasurably more potent than husbands, while maids are a great deal more fun than wives. Where sex is concerned, there is no such thing as Political Correctness. Then there is the Fun in a Brothel novel (when even less plotting is demanded – you can simply rely on the characters who turn up to be entertained, and without having to find any excuse for the appearance of more or less surprising sexual predilections). Your chief purpose is to provide overt sexual scenes every few pages; the way in which they are linked is secondary. Though a strong plot is certainly an advantage, no-one is going to base a thesis on the weakness of the narrative in Anon's *Eros in the Far East*. Really, anything goes, and the same may be said for the characters. It is desirable to have one or two who can make their way through the entire book and who have some excuse (however slender) for doing so. But on the whole you can allow characters to come and go as freely as they may wish: their motives can be as slender as you like – for you know and the reader knows that their only reason for being there at all is to interest the reader by satisfying their sexual urges.

Always remember that while in a conventional novel you can afford to elaborate the plot, surprise the reader and maybe yourself, in an erotic novel anticipation is a great part of the pleasure. If a character arrives at an hotel, is shown to his room by a maid whose figure is lovingly described as she mounts the stairs ahead of him, and if on arriving at his room she asks if she should run him a bath, neither he nor your reader will be surprised to find her in it when he opens the bathroom door. Should an innocent young maid recruited into an Eastern harem find the muscular torso of one of the guards strangely disturbing, few readers will be amazed when, on turning the page, he is discovered offering to demonstrate to her the strength of his arm.

Metaphor

This is not to say however that you need or should avoid subtlety: just as in the cinema there can be a world of sensuality in visual images, so in an erotic novel (or a novel that must be highly sexually charged) you can use symbolism and metaphor to make your effects. Most people will remember the scene in Tony Richardson's film of Fielding's *Tom Jones* in which Tom and Mrs Waters seduced each other during the course of a meal, the food and wine being consumed with such a wealth of amorous inference that by the end of the scene it would have been quite superfluous for the camera to follow them into the bedroom: we already knew why they would go there and what they would do when they got there. In a pornographic film of course it would be obligatory to follow them into bed; had that happened in *Tom Jones* it would have made the film unlicenceable – but in any case the seduction scene made any overt sexuality unnecessary: it is a rare case of an *hors d'oeuvre* being sufficiently nourishing to make the prospect of any more food unattractive.

In a novel, such effects are a little more difficult to achieve, and in conventional novels are sometimes so subtle that they pass some readers by. In his great novel *Buddenbrooks*, for instance, Thomas Mann wanted to hint at the dawning decadence of his young hero Hanno, still in his early teens, and hit on piano-playing as a metaphor for masturbation. Hanno's friend Kai asks him

'"Will you play this afternoon?"
'Hanno was silent a moment. A flush came upon his face, and a painful, confused look.
'"Yes, I'll play – I suppose – though I ought not. I ought to practise my sonatas and études and then stop. But I suppose I'll play; I cannot help it, though it only makes everything worse. . ."'

Mann's meaning must still elude many readers; this is always a risk with metaphor. However, it often has its effect subconsciously, even if the reader does not realise precisely what is going on. There is a marvellous little scene in Daudet's *Sappho*, for instance. Jean Gaussin, a young student, meets a woman at a costume ball: he takes her back to his rooms, which are up four flights of stairs in the Rue Jacob, and offers to carry her up:

'"Would you like me to carry you?" he asked, laughing, though softly in this sleeping house. . . And with the lovely fierce energy of youth and of the South he came from, he took her up in his arms and carried her like a child; he was sturdy and strapping, for all his girlish fair skin, and he went up the first flight without stopping for breath, rejoicing in his burden and the two beautiful, bare, rosy arms linked round his neck.
'The second flight was longer, less delightful. The woman let herself go, and weighed more heavily. The iron of her dangling ornaments, which was at first a caressing, a tickling of his skin, began to prick more cruelly and enter into his flesh.
'On the third flight he was gasping like a furniture remover shifting a piano. He was too breathless to speak, while she, with fluttering eyelids, rapturously murmured: "Oh, sweetheart, how lovely. . . how I do enjoy this. . ." And the last steps, which he climbed one at a time, were like the treads of a giant staircase and the walls, banisters and narrow windows seemed to be turning in an endless spiral. . .
'When they reached the narrow landing – "So soon?" she said, opening her eyes. What he thought was: "At last!"'

No-one surely can be in much doubt what is going on here – the symbolism is so obvious; but it is also a beautifully, tenderly comic scene which makes its effect however naive the reader.

To return to your initial conception of the story of your book, there is another reason why apart from the sex, and the preparations for sex, you should keep your plot relatively simple, as I have already suggested: there is in fact going to be little room to develop it (the same is true of characterisation). Your characters will spend most of the time in overt sexual activity, and scenes in which they must occupy themselves in working out some intricacy of the storyline will not be welcome. You should probably be able to set out a reasonable summary of your plot in one sentence, or certainly on one side of a postcard.

However, it is always useful to set it out chapter by chapter, so that you can make sure that you can get at least one or two sex scenes in each chapter. You might end up with something like:

The Amorous Valet.

Plot summary

Edwardian London. Young lad offered post as valet by Rich Young Bounder. R.Y.B. travels round England attempting to win bet by seducing one virgin every week for three months. Valet, employed by other party in bet, outwits master by getting to each girl first.

Chapter One Valet arrives at Park Lane house; new master interviews him while in bath with mistress (romp). Valet meets other servants; has to share room with young under butler; they entertain two maids from neighbouring bedroom (romp). Master places bet; tells valet; they set off for Bath.

But why Edwardian London? Why not 1990s London? Well, there is no really cogent or forceful reason; but it is not for nothing that most erotic books are set in a period not our own (though for some reason I have not quite fathomed, this is rarely the case with gay erotica, written for either sex). It is, quite simply, easier to fantasize about life in a more or less remote age, when we can pretend at least that our own sexual hang-ups or the proscriptions of society did not exist. In real life, the very opposite is of course the case: various sexual practises which are now common once resulted in prosecution and severe punishment, and not so long ago. Oscar Wilde was sent to gaol for having sex with a number of rent boys; not long before, he could have been executed for sodomy. Similarly, AIDS was unknown in 1820, but men died slowly and painfully from other sexually transmitted diseases. It is still for some reason which may be more psychological than real, easier to write about uninhibited sex in (or out of) costume than in modern dress or undress.

Take it off!

Until comparatively recently there was a very considerable emphasis on clothing in erotic novels. This probably dates from the Victorian period, when the only women many men ever saw entirely naked were likely to be prostitutes. The view that nudity was improper, even between lovers, was prevalent until relatively recently – the ubiquitous Mr Griffith-Jones, summing up in the Lady Chatterley case, was outraged at D. H. Lawrence's descriptions of Connie's breasts, before Mellors and she made love: 'Why introduce a little striptease into it all? What is the point of taking off the nightdress?'

Now, the naked body holds no mystery for the most casual television viewer, and though political correctness insists that a man who 'undresses a woman with his eyes' (or, presumably, the other way round) is committing some kind of offence, there is little inhibition about shedding one's clothes come bedtime. Research suggests that while a hundred years ago pornographers banged on about corsets and frilly knickers ad nauseam, very few men now get much pleasure from reading in detail about women's under-clothing (a mercy to those writers whose research in that area has been limited).

Individuals of course have their own fetishes; but though Tolstoy is said to have sat up in bed the night after finishing *War and Peace* with the horrified exclamation: 'My God! – I forgot to put in a yacht race!', an erotic novelist really can't be expected to cater for every obsession of his readers.

Who does what and to whom?

Your heroes and heroines must copulate in one setting or another, and indeed the setting, while it may not in itself be of much interest, can help with the real business of the book. Set your story in a school and it will be easier to introduce scenes of flagellation, if that is what you think turns your readers on; a bath-house dispenses with clothes and inhibitions; an Eastern setting has often allowed authors to inflict considerable pain and discomfort on heroines by the use of whips, labial clamps and nipple rings. Which brings us to the question of who does what, and with which, and to whom, as the limerick puts it.

While you can work out the moves, plan the game, in erotic prose perhaps more than in any other kind of writing except perhaps poetry, the unconscious must be allowed to take over. The writer can almost afford to fly on automatic pilot: set up the characters, make them ready for the battle and allow them free rein. Dreams, incidentally, can be a great help, if you instruct them to be so: think about your book just before you go to sleep and await developments. You will often find you wake from a dream which has given a twist to events of the plot in just the way you want or need (this is good advice when writing any kind of fiction, as Graham Greene knew).

Having said this, it is of course necessary to avoid monotony and repetition: but in that respect your initial scenario will help. In the example on page 66, I have simply written 'romp' to indicate a sexual scene and you can certainly do that when roughing out your plot. But you may well find, at first, that you should make a brief note on each romp. It is astonishing in how many erotic novels the sexual revels on page 10 are indistinguishable from those on page 176. That is silly, not only from the point of view of boring the reader, but psychologically – characters must have a sexual identity which is at least as strong as their physical and emotional identity: to have your hero make straight for his mistress' breasts on one occasion and ignore them on another is as stupid as to make this his first move on each subsequent occasion. On the other hand, of course, you could make breasts his 'thing' and build a whole novel on this particularly predilection (though it might not be easy).

The point is to hold the reader's attention, a good erotic novel should have considerable sexual variety; your 'automatic pilot' will in due course become expert at this; but at first you probably need consciously to contrive it.

How minute should the detail be in your sex scenes? Again, this is a matter of instinct – but in general, the answer must be that detail is a great help when it comes to avoiding monotony. Readers soon tire of scenes which merely repeat the obvious descriptions of thrusting buttocks and yielding thighs. It is also the case, of course, that descriptive details can make your characters more alive in the mind of the reader.

Those people who dislike or condemn pornography, vivid erotic scenes on television or in conventional fiction, often simply say 'You don't need all that detail', or 'But we don't need to see *that*'. The word 'need' is interesting: it could be argued that we don't *need* to see the loving detail – pictures, ornaments, food, period make-up – with which a Merchant Ivory film is invested, or the splendid landscape in which a BBC producer might set an adaptation of *Wuthering Heights*. But I suppose it might be argued that without it, we would lose something. Similarly, we would find Thomas Hardy less impressive without his descriptions of the Wessex landscape and Dickens less amusing without the vivid sense of caricature which makes his characters live in the mind's eye.

Is there a real difference between this, and a reader's expectation of detail in an erotic novel? It *is* important to know who is doing what to whom, and in as sensuous and exciting detail as you can provide. Some erotic novelists are better at this than others. Like every craft, it can of course to an extent be learned, partly by example and partly by practise. One woman novelist to whom I spoke told me that she found that her descriptions of love-making could never penetrate beyond the romantic to the pornographic; so she bought herself two or three pornographic videos, settled down and attempted to translate into prose what she saw on the screen. She has now published four extremely popular titles.

Virtual reality

Books in which men and women talk about their sexuality (a number have now been published) are also extremely helpful – in, for instance, enabling a man to discover as nearly as possible what it feels like for a woman to have an orgasm; while the actual sensation may be much the same, the approach and reaction are different. Don't think you can just skate over the surface of these matters: the closer you can get to reality, through observation or research, the better.

The same is true of the actual action in your sex scenes: you cannot be too minute in your attention to detail – it is what your reader has been waiting for, and to deny it to him or her would be like presenting to an Albert Hall audience a professional boxing match in which the contestants wore body armour. There would be a riot, and quite right too.

Who does what to whom, and where – much more importantly than why – must be the crux of every chapter of your book and you cannot describe it too comprehensively. This, unless your own sexual experience has been unlimited, means research as well as imagination. Books of men's and women's fantasies, as well as books on sexual technique (more or less professionally written – and some of them are clearly written for much the same purpose as that which has started you on your career) are helpful, as are films and videos and even 'girlie' (and 'boysie') magazines. To make the simplest point, the genitalia are almost as varied in appearance as the face – stupid to ignore the fact and not play upon it.

You will not be wasting time by describing and characterising your main protagonists in as much detail as you can, both erotically and in cooler blood. Who would argue that Fanny Hill's description of her lover (see p.30), which is entirely innocent of lubricious detail, does not make him and her feelings for him more real, and therefore enhances the descriptions of their love making?

Violence

Violence in erotic fiction is by no means the prerogative of men – any reader who feels that only men are interested in the subjugation and brutalization of women should turn to Pauline Réage's *Story of O* (more recently, Cleo Cordell's *The Senses Bejewelled* has much to say of clitoral rings, labia clamps, whips and chains). Interestingly enough, those erotic books written particularly for women and published for instance under the Black Lace imprint seem to contain even more scenes of male domination than those written for men. Nancy Friday, in the anthology of male fantasies she published under the title *Men in Love* (1980), remarks that 'in my books on women's sexual fantasies, the single greatest theme that emerged was that of "weak" women being sexually dominated, "forced" by male strength to do this deliciously awful thing, made to perform that marvellously forbidden act, guiltlessly "raped" again and again.' Only a fool would suggest that any woman actually wants to be raped; but the suggestion seems to be that she enjoys reading about it. A great number of erotic books by and for women contain a high incidence of rape, suggesting that the dominant, sadistic male is a highly attractive character, at least in the world of fantasy. *In the fiction they read* (and those words cannot of course be too strongly emphasised), *in fiction* women do enjoy rape. (I should for my own protection say that this statement is based entirely on the evidence collected by publishers; I would not personally have put it forward as a theory, and indeed found it initially difficult to believe).

Contrarily, and despite the popular belief, male fantasies of forcing women against their will are exceptional, and those writers who highlight this kind of sexual behaviour in their male characters when writing erotic books for men, make a big mistake. This does not mean that the idea of force does not appeal to men as to women – but the kind of force male readers enjoy reading about is that which is offered to a woman by a man who knows she actually enjoys it. Similarly, the point of flagellation (in real life as well as in fiction) is that the recipient enjoys it as much as the protagonist – the whipped man or woman is invariably aroused to the point of orgasm; the woman who is raped ends up by enjoying sex more than she has ever done before. So those who protest against even the grimmest scene of sadism or masochism in a novel may (except in the grimmest and least defensible cases) have hold of the wrong end of the cane: scenes of rape and other forms of sexual violence *in fiction* do not necessarily express hostility to women or outrageous misogyny, but a wish to give as well as receive sexual pleasure.

Whether such scenes, in a book, are likely to provoke actual violence against women is another matter. The evidence is inconclusive, and debaters on both sides in the argument can produce statistics which support their views. My own instinct is that books describing violence, even of the most offensive kind, probably act as a catharsis rather than encouraging readers to emulate the characters who go about raping and pillaging, torturing and killing.

The most extreme example of such books are, of course, those of the Marquis de Sade. His novels have always seemed to me to belong to the history of pathology rather than of literature (though there are those who will argue for his merit as an author); I find them repulsive, and I cannot say that I would be mortified if by some generous act of nature they were all to disappear overnight. However, there seems to me to be no firm evidence that they have ever driven anyone to emulate the actions of their protagonists; they have certainly been found in the possession of sadists, some of whom have committed murder – but to the question which came first, the sadistic impulse or the literature that mirrored it, there is no proven answer. Certainly the violent acts of de Sade himself were committed before he *wrote* the books, which – like many dissimilar works – have frequently been used as aids to masturbation and therefore the release of sexual tensions (which might otherwise have led to overt expression).

Every writer who turns to erotic fiction must of course consider these matters for him- or herself, and reach a decision about them: just as s/he must decide just how far to go in describing specific actions which might be dangerous to health if by any chance some reader unthinkingly emulated them.

Your readers

What do we know about the people who read erotic books and about their taste in them? It is a difficult question to answer. The short answer is that all sorts of men and women read and enjoy pornography. But Virgin, the publishers of the Nexus books for men and the Black Lace books for women, have done a little research from which they have kindly allowed me to quote. This suggests that about half the readers of the Nexus books left full-time education before they were sixteen and have a household income of less than £20,000 a year. This is very different from the social and economic situation of women readers of erotica (see pp.48-9), and, one suspects, different too from the buyers of conventional novels and non-fiction, who are probably on average somewhat better educated.

But the picture is not a simple one, and as Virgin points out 'Nexus readers are not *Sun* readers. . . they buy books out of choice, they are literate and intelligent.' And they remind us also that of the remaining 50 per cent of Nexus book-buyers, a large proportion has an income in excess of £40,000 a year. The lesson, clearly, is not ever to write down to them.

The believable fantasy

Male readers, it is claimed, want fantasies which are 'just about believable'; they must be able to persuade themselves fairly easily that what is going on is at least remotely possible: the fantasy, in other words, must be easy to enter into. But remember that it is not a good idea, in your quest to create a real background or setting for the fantasy, to weigh it down with too much detail. Setting an erotic novel in, say, the convict settlements of nineteenth century Australia may be a very good idea: but providing detailed statistics about the man-woman ratio on the convict ships, or describing in detail the social structure of Melbourne in 1860, can very easily indeed bore a reader who has picked up the book expecting something rather earthier.

One reader in five who buys a Nexus book is said to be a woman, but the editors suggest that writers should forget this: 'mention erect willies by all means,' they say, 'but don't waste words on loving descriptions. Men want to read about women.' It is fair to say that not all publishers of erotic fiction feel that way; some books ostensibly written for men, but including some chapters from a female point of view, have sold very well. A man might be reluctant to buy a book with a naked man, or even an embracing couple, on the cover; but it is not necessarily the case that he will shrink from overt homosexual scenes in the book itself – whether from curiosity or a simple exercise of the normal but suppressed feminine instincts in every man, is a moot point. It is probably worth remembering that two out of five men are said to have had some homosexual contact during their lives, and not all of them disliked it.

Discussing what readers want, Nexus editors suggest that 'the most popular sub-interests of male readers' (the main interest presumably being in 'straight' descriptions of coitus); 'are in the area of bondage and discipline, with lesbianism as the next most requested speciality.' (The history of erotic fiction in English certainly confirms this proposition, and a look at the cards displayed inside a Soho telephone kiosk seems to support it). 'It's a good idea to include a few such scenes even in a novel which has no particular slant or has a different slant.'

The editors can't resist a little medical instruction: 'Take care with anatomical descriptions – it is quite astounding how many men are confused about the positioning of female genitalia. Female orgasm is triggered in most instances by clitoral stimulation. The clitoris is not situated inside or adjacent to the vagina.' (This reminds one of the splendidly chauvinistic joke about the alleged difference between a clitoris and a pub: nine out of ten Australian men can find a pub.) 'Also, women do not produce copious amounts of sexual secretions on orgasm.' Well, one comment on this is that any writer ambitious to write erotic fiction who does not inform himself about simple anatomical detail should turn his hand to writing books on elementary carpentry; and another is that several erotic novels written by women are full of descriptions in which the heroines liberally bedew the hero and the adjacent bed-linen with 'sexual secretions'; so a little licence is being taken somewhere.

Black Lace

The Black Lace books, written by women for women, despite being produced with cool deliberation as 'aids to arousal and masturbation' are 'positioned slightly up-market of male-oriented erotic fiction. We expect them to sell less strongly than male-oriented erotic fiction at travel points, but more strongly in the High Street bookshops and newsagents. As women's fiction, they can be sold alongside romances without anyone batting an eye.' And so they are.

The desirable settings for Black Lace books are said to be 'fairly realistic', and the characters should be 'well-drawn. . . engaged with each other in a realistic, or at least very believable, setting' – though it is suggested that readers 'do not like to be reminded constantly of domesticity', and 'don't want to read about husbands, difficult relationships, or men with impotence and other sexual problems.' Again, exceptions can of course always be made: one Black Lace novel at least has a co-hero severely affected by an injury which has made him semi-impotent: the heroine's achievement being of course to help him overcome the problem.

Rather surprisingly, research suggests that readers prefer contemporary locations; while writers on the other hand seem to favour period settings. There doesn't seem to be any way of solving that problem, which happily isn't fatal to the success of a book which is satisfactory in other respects.

The advice on plot tallies very much with what I have already suggested: 'the story gives the reader another reason for turning the pages: she wants to find the next dirty bit, of course, but she should also be intrigued about what happens next.'

Under the heading of 'sex' the advice is, again, fairly predictable. 'Your plot, settings and characters should not be allowed to sideline the important stuff: frequent and detailed descriptions of sexual activity.' The editors admit that 'some of our readers would be satisfied with a series of repetitive descriptions of well-endowed couples bonking', but go on to suggest that this is really rather dull (for the writer as well as the reader, goodness knows), and proposes that different settings, varied characters, unconventional clothing and bizarre props will help to vary the scenes.

Here come the actors

Just as a play begins when the actors enter the stage, so it is probably true of most novels that they originate when the characters stroll into the writer's mind. A writer may think that a book set on the *Titanic* or during the American Civil War or a British election campaign may be a good idea; but nothing will come of it until a man or a woman presents himself, tugs at your sleeve and announces that s/he is the one who is going to stride through the events of the book. You will be well advised to get some clear idea of your character or characters before you start.

The hero or heroine of an erotic novel needs, whatever the period and whatever the story, to be what Freud called polymorphous perverse. In infancy, tiny babies receive erotic pleasure from everything they do or that is done for them – from feeding to being cuddled, from touching animals to being bathed, from warmth, from feeling a warm breeze on their skin, from actual masturbation and from attention to every orifice of the body. The erotic writer will do well to remember this kind of pleasure and this kind of freedom, and to assume that his characters will exercise it: at least, eventually – a large number of erotic novels have dealt with the innocent hero or more often heroine who gradually becomes addicted to all kinds of sexual activity as a result of the strenuous inventiveness of the hero (or indeed the villain) who introduces her to it.

Remember always that a reader comes to an erotic book in search of an illustration or extension of his or her fantasy life. Fantasies represent the forbidden, and we often unconsciously rebuke ourselves for them – people are extremely anxious about dreams in which they have watched or taken part in some action which is taboo, but to which they are unconsciously attracted. Erotic novels bring the taboo onto the page and present it shamelessly to the reader. It is in this respect that, if they are good, they will very probably improve the sex life of couples who read them together.

However, on the whole they are read alone and as an aid to masturbation (happily, no longer a reprehensible practise); since there are, to coin a phrase, different strokes for different folks, it is an advantage – even a necessity – for the writer as well as the hero and heroines of erotic fiction to be, at least in theory, polymorphous perverse: that is, at least to be prepared to contemplate every conceivable form of sexuality. Occasionally one overhears a writer say, 'Well, I thought I might write an erotic novel – there seems to be quite a lot of money in it,' and in the next breath to profess a deep distaste for some particular aspect of sex. This won't do. The writer who makes a success of writing erotica will be interested in sex, enjoy it and be unshocked by any manifestation of it. S/he will *not* be disturbed by homosexuality or bestiality or fetishism, though s/he may well thoroughly disapprove of cruelty or force.

You don't have to approve of every aspect of sex, or write about it; there are the strongest arguments for not writing about sex with under-age children, for instance; and one should be careful, in my view, when writing about violent sex (see also pp.105-6). But a would-be writer of erotic books who is too repelled by – let's say – the very idea of cunnilingus or sodomy to be able to think about them without disgust, is starting out at such a disadvantage that s/he might as well give up right away. Neither, of course, should you be delicate about language: you must be ready to call a spade a spade (and the Wildean excuse that you have never seen a spade will not do!)

Let them alone

But to return to your characters: once they have formed in your mind, you will usually find that they suggest their own plot, or at least their own settings, and that they behave with a very considerable degree of independence. All writers of fiction have experienced that strange moment when a character decides to go in the opposite direction to that which you, his creator, intended. Non-writers tend not to believe that this can happen; but of course it does – just as other characters may stride into a room unannounced, without your invitation, and demand a piece of the action. If they do, let them alone to get on with dictating your book to you.

Clearly, their intervention is the result of the enormous part played in the creation of fiction by the writer's unconscious. The unexpected action of a main character, or the sudden appearance of someone you seem not to know, is far from random: you have been working on it without knowing it, and probably for some time. The advantage of writing an erotic novel is that you can usually afford to give your **characters their heads** without worrying too much about how this is going to affect the development of the book. It is probably unnecessary to work out a plot too strictly in the first place. If a character suddenly decides to go off to South America, you can often afford to let her do it, with no more harm done than providing you with the little problem of contriving to work the trip into the general shape of the book.

Hero and heroine

You cannot allow yourself quite the same freedom in choosing your hero or heroine as if you are contemplating an ordinary novel – but the parameters are not as narrow as you might think. There is no reason why your hero should not have a developed character rather than being the simple rutting stag of so many Victorian pornographic novels – any more than your heroine need be a busty hoyden or a caricature cat. But it is probably unwise to make him or her too complex. Your character's chief motivation, remember, is his or her sexual drive (and by the way if women readers will forgive me, I will from now simply for convenience on allude only to a hero, though the rules apply also if the main character in your book is a woman).

In another kind of book a character's psychological sexual profile could certainly be a major focus of interest for both writer and reader. In an erotic novel things are simpler: your character's duty is to manoeuvre himself into a regular succession of sexual situations. His reason for jumping into bed with this woman or that should – or at any rate need – not primarily be psychological, but physiological. Otherwise you will find yourself spending more and more time on his mind, when what readers are interested in is his body and what he is doing with it.

There doesn't seem to be a requirement to exclude any kind of character from an erotic novel, though clearly the reader needs to identify with the hero or heroine, who should therefore be as nearly as possible an 'average' man or woman (though keeping in mind the necessity for him to have a voracious sexual appetite). In films, there has recently (at last, one might add) been recognition that the elderly or physically disabled can have a satisfactory and satisfying sex life; I have yet to read an erotic novel with a disabled hero or heroine, but there is absolutely no reason why one should not be written. The writer would have to be brave and sensitive to the situation; but there would be no inherent objection to the theme itself. Similarly, the idea that sex does not apply to the over-sixties has taken a satisfactory beating in recent years, and though a writer might not automatically fix on a pensioner as his hero, again there is no argument against it. As with every other kind of writing, if you can bring the trick off, and it works, then we shall all applaud; fail, and – well, you just fail, and that's that.

Your main characters should of course be consistent at least in basic characteristics: a woman should not have blue eyes on page 3, and brown ones on page 101; a man should not express a preference for blondes in the first chapter and brunettes in the forth. Their sexuality, too, should be consistent, however exuberant they are: though there is no reason why they should not be changed by their experiences. A heroine who dislikes pain may be tied up and whipped and find the experience delightfully arousing; indeed this has happened so often that it is now a cliché which one would do best to avoid.

In writing a thriller or a conventional romance, you can cast your hero or heroine (the terms are probably misleading: your central characters let's say) in whatever mould you like – you can have a rather tetchy, humourless hero; or one who is in some way unappealing. In an erotic novel, though you can have one or two repulsive characters, your main character must be not merely acceptable to your readers but positively appealing. It is best if the reader can identify with him or her, at least to some extent. Reading a James Bond thriller, we may persuade ourselves that we are performing his more dangerous stunts – but Ian Fleming was so bad at writing sex scenes that one does not get much of a chance to identify with him while he is bedding his various girls. In an erotic novel, it is best if we can identify with the protagonists: there is no point in fantasy if one cannot live inside it. It could be argued that the skeletonal nature of Fleming's sex scenes at least allow the reader to exercise his own imagination – but that is not, in this context, the point; and anyway, you will do best to assume that you are writing for those whose imaginations are perhaps less lively than yours.

There are plenty of pornographic novels in which this is not the case: in which the characters are simply lay figures, good for a lay and not much else. In the better erotic novels, they are more: Fanny Hill is a very real character, and her lover (though less fully characterised) a real man. So while you have to invest your characters with the necessary and usually unattainable virtues or attributes necessary to their task – the men must be vigorous stallions, the women enthusiastic recipients of their attentions – it is profitable to make them much more than mere rutting animals.

Their characters can – probably must – be developed during the overt sex scenes, if only because there's not a great deal of space elsewhere. So, for instance, if your view is that an erotic novel will sell best in which the men are Men, the hero's attitude to the women he beds will reflect that; whereas if you feel that many of your prospective male audience now possess a rather less simple attitude to women, you can afford to develop their feminine side – making them more caring, more intent in pleasuring their companions. This will also please, and may attract, women readers, thus enlarging your sales.

Bisexuality?

There is a strong case to be made for the writer of erotic fiction to be bisexual in his or her approach. Throughout the history of English erotic literature pornography written for men has always contained lesbian scenes and very often scenes of male homosexuality. The first are readily understandable: the idea of two women making love has played a part in male fantasies since Greek and Roman times, and no doubt earlier. It is rather more surprising that even in ages when male homosexuality has been condemned, not only by the law but by public opinion (and the two are not always synonymous), erotic novels and short stories produced for male consumption have featured it. In some books, with that hypocrisy which has always been a feature of the British attitude to sex, the writer describes gay lovemaking with great enthusiasm, only to add the information that it is, of course, nauseous to all right-thinking people.

In *Fanny Hill* the single homosexual scene was deleted from some editions – and in the original, Fanny allegedly meant to denounce the lovers to the police, but was prevented from doing so by an unfortunate accident. This was Cleland covering his back, as it were. But in one of the most popular serials in the Victorian erotic magazine *The Pearl, Sub-Umbra, or sport among the She-Noodles* (a splendidly politically incorrect title) the young male narrator and his cousin Frank seem to be almost as happy exploring each other's sexuality (in 'an extasy of delight') as that of their female cousins. More often, perhaps, the homosexual scenes were between an elderly *roué* and a young man; but both parties were usually shown to be enjoying themselves – and this twenty years before Oscar Wilde was sent to Reading Gaol for exercises much less adventurous than those described in *The Pearl*, or even in *Teleny*, the novel he may have helped to write, and almost certainly edited.

Clearly all this sheds an interesting light on Victorian attitudes to sex. In our own time, certainly in the last twenty years, writers of erotic literature have explored bisexuality more freely and uninhibitedly. It is now far more common to see two men greeting each other with a hug and even a kiss, than it used to be. There has always been a tendency to view lesbianism as perhaps regrettable but understandable – now, male homosexuality is also becoming less of a moral issue, and many men reject the ruthless definition of masculine gender identity which so inhibited their fathers' generation. While some men still emerge from possible youthful experiment with homosexuality to live a wholly heterosexual life, they are no longer shamed of or horrified to remember their earlier experiences, and, more self-assured and secure about their own sexual identity, are more tolerant of ambiguities, and often happy to experience them by proxy.

Interestingly, while lesbian scenes appear not only in erotic novels written by men, but those written by and for women, homosexual scenes have so far very rarely appeared in the latter. It is difficult to explain why; it is simply a fact. But tastes may of course change and the new attempts to write erotic books which will appeal both to men and women may help to change them.

This new freedom does not of course meant that your hero must necessarily leap as readily into bed with other men as with the women, but it certainly frees them to do so – and you should certainly be aware that all men have their feminine side just as women have their male side, and that both can be profitably developed in your characters, not only in flagrant action but in attitude and emotion.

Real love

It is important not be deceived into believing that there is no place for emotion in an erotic novel. The word 'love' is by no means taboo; and in general – that is, for the majority of readers – the belief that in the end a sexual act performed with love is infinitely preferable to one performed out of simple lust, is important. Most readers, the huskiest of men, prefer it that way: the majority dream of sex with a loving partner, which is why even the most rank pornographic novel often ends 'happily' – with at least a final loving sexual act to round off the book with a sensation of contentment, of fulfilment.

Research

My wife and I once prepared an anthology on the subject of love, and I remarked in a TV interview that the research had been very tiring. Researching for erotic novels might be a great deal more so. (I must say I long for the moment when an author produces to the

Inspector of Taxes a dozen receipts from the world's best and most expensive brothels and attempts to claim a tax allowance.)

There are happily a number of ways in which to research your subject without injuring either your health or your personal relationship. The most obvious is via the bookshelves (not always the library bookshelves, for libraries still have an equivocal attitude to erotica, though this varies somewhat according to the outlook of individual librarians).

It is a good idea to avoid reading too many contemporary erotic novels.

You should certainly look at a few, particularly those published by any firm to which you are thinking of submitting your own work (though do take care to note when the book you have in your hand was published – not only the public's taste but the requirement of the publishers may alter considerably in five or ten years: fashion is as fickle in this area as in any other). But while it may well be wise to approximate the tone of your own book to that of others on the contemporary scene, be careful not to copy either style or content slavishly. Put yourself in the place of the reader: having enjoyed a book by writer A, you don't specially want to buy an imitation of her work. You want a book by writer B which is equally enjoyable in its own way. This should not need saying, but alas it does.

To return to the subject of research: anthologies of sexual fantasy such as Nancy Friday's *Men in Love* and *Women on Top* are very valuable – probably more valuable than any other kind of book – not only because they may kick-start an idea of your own for a scene, or even a complete novel, but because they will help to destroy any idea you may have that your own fantasies are likely to be too strong for your readers. This is extremely unlikely. There is, in this field as in every other, nothing new under the sun. Your own imagination may carry you very successfully through your first book or two, but if you are thinking of erotica as a regular source of income, you will probably find that your imagination needs some kind of stimulus, from time to time, if you are not to repeat yourself to an extent that you will bore both your readers and yourself. You may find pornographic videos, soft- or hard-, useful in the same way. If you hesitate to visit your local sex shop, the small ads columns of the local and some national newspapers usually carry advertisements for these.

Such books as the Kinsey reports on human sexuality are valuable; more off-beat books such as the *Illustrated Book of Sexual Records* may well be useful not only for ideas but for light relief (and see p.107). It is also useful to keep a file of relevant clippings from newspapers and magazines – the women's magazines are particularly fruitful ground to tread: the frequent surveys to which their readers reply ('which part of the male anatomy most attracts you to a man', and so on) are full of useful information and tips!

The sex manual

Any writer of erotic fiction would be delighted to have achieved the worldwide sales of that remarkable book *The Joy of Sex*, first published in 1972, and written by the sexologist and poet Alex Comfort. No doubt part of the book's success was due to the frankness of the illustrations; but it was a book which was published at precisely the right moment. Or one might almost say republished, for its like has appeared from time to time over the centuries. Ovid's *Art of Love* – a textbook on the art of seduction and pleasure – came out two thousand years ago. An even more famous erotic manual was the *Kama Sutra of Vatsyayana*, written perhaps between the first and fourth century AD, translated by Sir Richard Burton and first published in England in 1885 – its republication in 1963 resulted in enormous sales.

The *Kama Sutra* was originally a religious work: the union of men and women was conceived by the Hindus as the symbol of divine creation, and Vatsyayana claimed to have written his book 'while leading the life of a religious student and wholly engaged in the contemplation of the Deity.' Acts which were (and in some places still are) regarded as shameful, are celebrations of the divine spirit of man, translated into terms of sensuality.

It would be silly to suppose that the *Kama Sutra* is a sex manual in the practical sense: those few Victorian men who were able, at some expense, to acquire a copy may well have improved their sex lives (and hopefully, the sex lives of their wives) as a result of reading it – they would almost certainly have read of practises of which they were unaware. But after all, many of the postures recommended are far too acrobatic for the most lithe of Western lovers, and even the early twentieth century western sex manuals were rather more helpful to their readers.

As erotic literature, however, the *Kama Sutra* has always been a great success in the West. Burton (1821-1890) invented the largely fictional Kama Shastra Society (of London and Benares) in order to issue the book 'for private subscribers only'. He dedicated it 'to that small portion of the British public which takes enlightened interest in studying the manners and customs of the olden east.' The book immediately became the prized possession of those interested in 'curious literature', but it was only made available to the ordinary book-buying public in the second half of the century, when the bonds of censorship were loosed (meanwhile, Burton's widow had understandably but unforgivably burned over a thousand pages of his other translations of Indian erotic writing).

It immediately sold like hot cakes, partly because it came out at a time when 'respectable' erotica (that is, erotic books which could be carried openly, clad in their own dust-jackets, without too much scandal being provoked) was rare. Readers who had not found it easy to come by such books found that their appetite grew by what it fed on. As Vatsyayana himself put it: 'The whole subject of embracing is of such a nature that men who ask questions about it, or who hear about it, or who talk about it, acquire thereby a desire for enjoyment. Even those embraces that are not in the Kama Sutra should be practised at the time of sexual enjoyment, if they are in any way conducive to the increase of love or passion. . .'

Elegance and poetry

The appeal of the *Kama Sutra* was not only in its overt descriptions of sexual activity, but in a certain literary elegance and poetry. English and American readers were interested to speculate on the possibility of reproducing some of the postures described:

> 'When a woman, having placed one of her feet on the foot of her lover, and the other on one of his thighs, passes one of her arms round his back, and the other on his shoulders, makes slightly the sounds of singing and cooing, and wishes, as it were, to climb up him in order to have a kiss, it is called an embrace like "the climbing of a tree".'

But inter alia, the book was certainly educative, even for readers who had not picked it up for use as a text-book (and that most have been most of them). There are, of course, other eastern texts which repay study – as a source of ideas no less than of good poetic sensual prose: two more were translated by Burton. *The Ananga-Ranga of Kalayana Malla* was written during the Indian Middle Ages, by which time women were no longer as free and equal as they had once been. It contains a bewildering number of hints – 'at the time of the New Moon the Hastini woman's yoni should be manipulated and pulled open like a flower' – and detailed instructions on the sexual use of every part of the body, from the big toe to the left ear. Later still comes the more famous *Perfumed Garden of Sheik Nefzawi*, written by a poet with a sense of humour: his list of names for 'the virile member' is delightful, ranging from The Creeper and The Exciter to The Stumbler and The Flabby One (which, sadly, 'gives no pleasure to a woman, for it only inflames her passions and cannot quench them').

We have already mentioned *L'Ecole des Filles* as an erotic book (see pages 25-7) and it is reasonable to suppose that education was not at the forefront of the author's mind when he wrote it. The book's disguise as a book of instruction and edification was an excuse – but then, would it be unfair to suppose that modern publishers, including those of *The Joy of Sex* (to say nothing of *More Joy* (1973) and *The Joy of Gay Sex* – the latter never published in England, though a great success in America before the AIDS era), resolutely rejected the idea that a book dealing in great detail with every aspect of sexuality might also sell well?

The 'educative' element of *L'Ecole des Filles* is considerable, and one can see that it might have been valuable as well as titillating for any young men or women who were able to catch the meaning. The contents of the two dialogues of which the book consists (summarised in the author's 'table of contents'), includes 'preliminary remarks for the instruction of girls in the art of love's delights', 'a discourse on the stones' (testicles), 'interior description of the cunt, which is the most difficult thing of all to investigate', 'an important lesson for girls in how to thrust with their bottoms' and 'why some postures are more enjoyable than others.'

The author lists no fewer than 145 separate topics for discussion and does cover most of them. Though it is clear that in dealing with those subjects he is at least as interested in arousing the reader's passion as in imparting information, he does actually provide the descriptions he promises:

> 'The two orbs which hang in a bag. . . are called his *stones*, though it would be improper to use that term in public. When you take them in your hand, you'll find they feel much like two large Spanish olives, but they are surrounded by curly hair just like that of a girl – hair which beautifies the surrounding region.'

The author of *L'Ecole* was by no means untalented, both as writer and as sexologist – one of the pleasures of the book is that Fanchon and Susanne, the two young girls who engage in the dialogue which makes up the book, are well characterised and in fact have a great deal of charm. His book, incidentally, contains nothing to suggest that he was a doctor, or had any more information than any intelligent man might gather for himself with the aid of a little personal research (though he did have an enlightened attitude to the subject, insisting for instance that a woman should receive as much pleasure as a man, and that a great part of a lover's duty was to ensure that she did so).

The author's modern equivalent is more likely than not to be a specialist in the physiology and psychology of sex – if only because most publishers demand it: the non-specialist writer who decided he wants to write a sex manual will have an uphill task selling it unless he can produce some good reason why a reader should accept the information and advice he gives. Alex Comfort is a doctor as well as a poet, and indeed the former occupation was more useful to him in writing *The Joy of Sex* than the latter. So, of course, was his personal interest in and enthusiasm for sex, and not least his decision to allow his name to be placed on the title page of a book which only a few years before its appearance would certainly have been considered an entirely improper volume to be written by a respectable doctor.

The romantic novel

But haven't I missed something out? Many writers still find sex the least important part of their novel – though one which cannot be ignored. They feel, very strongly, that 'showing' the reader what goes on in the bedroom is unnecessary and at worst gratuitous.

This is, it need hardly be said, as entirely respectable a point of view as that which finds overt sexuality permissable and in some circumstances desirable. But it presents some difficulty for the author concerned.

The writers who are likely to encounter most difficulty are perhaps those who write 'romances' – what used to be called 'Mills and Boon' novels, in which open sexuality was frowned upon. The past sense is obligatory, for that firm now publishes novels of every shade of sexuality from pure white to blazing scarlet. However, some writers now feel that a novel in which open sexuality plays no part must be regarded as 'old-fashioned', and would be difficult to sell – and they may have a point, for the judges of the valuable Betty Trask Award for a novel in the traditional *genre* have frequently given the award to books whose sexual scenes would (one may reliably assume) have considerably shocked its founder.

In every form of writing, excellence is its own salesman, and it is of course still possible to write a novel in which the power of sexual attraction is the mainspring, without overt sexual scenes playing a part in it – though it must be said that in the 1990s, it is very difficult. A contemporary author would now find it difficult to write *Wuthering Heights* without describing fairly graphically the love scenes between Cathy and Heathcliff – and were she alive no doubt Emily Brontë would take advantage of licence.

A writer's emotion always shows in his or her work, and embarrassment is certainly a case in point. If you feel embarrassed while you are writing a love scene, then you should seriously consider whether your book needs that scene, or needs it in the terms in which you are writing it. If you have to spend time wondering whether you 'can' or 'should' use certain words, whether such and such a phrase will offend your readers; if you do not know exactly what your characters would do in bed, and feel entirely free to describe it, then you are in real difficulty. It is time to consider whether your readers would not, perhaps like you, prefer to remain outside the bedroom door. There is nothing wrong with that, and it will be infinitely preferable to an erotic scene which betrays in every line its writer's shuddering embarrassment.

In such a case as this, you are most likely to be writing for a particular audience and probably have a particular publisher in mind. As with every other *genre*, it will be very well worth looking along the shelves for books similar in tone to your own, and carefully noting how the authors deal with this particular problem. There is, indeed, no other way in which you can make a decision; if the books contain explicit sexual scenes which you feel incapable of writing, you are aiming at the wrong market and the wrong publisher.

6
Erotic humour

I have written elsewhere about the dangers (see p.50) of allowing humour into erotic scenes; on the page as in bed, though sex can be fun, if it becomes *funny* there is perhaps something wrong somewhere. In erotic books it is certainly important to convey the fun; but remember that if you wish to deflate a man or a woman, laughing at them is the quickest and most effective way. In conventional novels, a comic scene involving sex is another matter, of course; but funny sex is not on the whole arousing – or it is very difficult to make it so.

There are a few, a very few, genuinely funny books which are erotic. It's a good trick if you can do it – but very few writers can. Perhaps the best-written largely humorous but erotic novel to come to mind is Gore Vidal's *Myra Breckinridge* (1968), the 'true confession' of a transsexual – a biting satire which manages at the same time to be funny and an aphrodisiac – as in the scene in which Myra, an outrageous drama teacher, once a man, sexually humiliates the true American college boy Rusty Godowsky – a scene in which an overtly sexual situation is treated with just the elegant wit one would expect of Vidal.

Candy (1958) and *Blue Movie* (1973) may not be so elegantly written, but they are even more outrageously funny, and with stronger erotic language: *Candy*, by Terry Southern and Mason Hoffenburg, was originally only published in a carefully expurgated edition; an unexpurgated text did not appear until 1970. As Julian Symons wrote in a review in the *Sunday Times*, 'Candy Christian is a wide-eyed American innocent, a genuine charmer . . . Her adventures with mystics, sexual analysts, doctors, are immensely funny and her innocence, in print as in action, really does make everything acceptable. *Candy*. . . is that rarity, a funny book about sex.'

Even in 1970 the publishers seem to have been somewhat worried about the possibility of prosecution, for the unexpurgated edition came out with a rather heavy defensive Introduction by Professor David Daiches, in which he suggests that 'its frankness in the description of sexual acts is made comic by style, so that the humour purges the pornography it is satirizing.' Well, yes and no; the satire is mainly directed at the doctors and analysts: it is difficult to believe that the authors did not thoroughly enjoy writing the sex scenes, and intend the readers to enjoy them. The tone of the book comes out in an early scene, in which the innocent Candy has invited the young Mexican gardener Emmanuel, who she feels in some obscure way 'needs her', to her room:

'"Oh, you do need me so!" the closed-eyed girl murmured, as yet not feeling much of anything. . . But when the gardener's hand closed on her pelvis and into the damp, she stiffened slightly: she was quite prepared to undergo *pain* for him. . . but *pleasure* – she was not sure how that could be a part of the general picture. So she seized his hand and contented herself for the moment with the giving of her left breast, to which his mouth was fastened in desperate sucking.

'"Oh my baby, my baby," she whispered, stroking his head; but the hot insulting hardness of him between her legs was distracting, and somehow destroyed the magic of her breast sacrifice. She closed her eyes again. . . "Oh how you ache for me, my darling." She flung both arms around his neck, as he found her tiny clitoris and pummelled it with his calloused fingers, causing her to cry out and stiffen once more in his arms; but now she fought down the desire to seize his hand, thinking how this was the prize of loveliness and the key to the beautiful thrilling privilege of giving fully. . .'

At this point however Candy's father enters, and interrupts them by having a heart attack. The comedy is of course in Candy's innocence, which despite its extremity is believably maintained throughout the book.

But read the whole novel and observe the skill with which humour fuses with eroticism and produces a work which is funny, arousing and genuinely satirical. *Blue Movie*, a satire on Hollywood and sex, is not perhaps quite so successful as a whole – but it is from time to time even funnier. Part of the book details the making of a pornographic film - in which the female star is determined to avoid actually having sex, but has agreed to perform fellatio on a replica of her partner's penis.

'Nicky, of course, had personally supervised the entire process, first taking a plaster-of-Paris impression of Feral's organ at full rigidity, then casting it in molten Latex with a flexible metal rod at its center. It was remarkably detailed, the surface seeming to pulsate with veins and taut sinews.

'"I'll tell you where it doesn't work," said Boris after considering it further, "at the *foreskin*. . . now watch what happens when she comes all the way up on it. . . Angie, dear, just bring your mouth all the way up, okay . . . that's it. . . now back down, slowly. . ." He turned to Nicky again, 'You see, since he's not circumcised it should pull the foreskin up just a little when her mouth reaches the end, then it should push it *down* a little when she takes it back in. But the trouble is, the foreskin doesn't *move* on a mould. You get the *contour*, the *definition* of the foreskin, but you don't get any *movement*. I mean, I had an idea for a beautiful image – where she puts her tongue under the foreskin and slowly moves it around the head. Get the picture?"

'"Oh, yes," said Nicky, huskily, "yes, I do, indeed."

'"Well, we can't do it with a mould – there's nothing for her tongue to go *under*." He sighed in frustration. "Why the hell won't she just *suck his cock* for a minute or two? What's so terrible about that?"

'"I simply cannot *imagine*," said Nicky arching his brows in great hauteur, ". . . the silly little goose."'

Robert Glover's *One Hundred Dollar Misunderstanding* (1961) is less well-known, but just as funny, narrated in alternative chapters by a WASP American boy and a young black prostitute called Kitten. The use of southern American dialect for comic effect in the sex scenes is clever and successful: there is no need for detailed description of what goes on:

'I wash him real nice an soff, count him bein so awful tickledingus, and then I gits t'work. Time I start in, I got me so many worryful considerins t'do, I can't hardly pay no mind t'techneek. Workin an considerin, an wonnerin does this dum Whiteboy know what t'do wiff that thing fer the other haff o'his haff and haff, I find I done me too dam much considerin.

'Nex, I ain been at him a minit, an pop, off he go!

'Kee-ryees!

'An then – I git up an go over t'the basin – this Whiteboy, he sit up like a mothahjumpin jack-in-a-box an he start lookin at me like I done somethin wrong.

'Gee-zuz! All that Jack an I can' make nothin go right, he so fuggin dum. Come in here all loaded up like that an I don' even git a chance t'show him how good I kin do. Naecher done mess me up at the most baddes time.

'An he still lookin, Gee-zus!

'Then he say, That all?'

Philip Roth's *Portnoy's Complaint* (1969) probably needs little introduction: it was the first novel to have masturbation as its central theme, though the British author Brian Aldiss later used it in his *The Hand-Reared Boy*, and to almost equal comic effect (though in a generally more serious book). While both Vidal and Southern have genuinely erotic scenes, Roth emphasises the humour – and very funny he is too. Here is Portnoy, the archetypical Jewish boy, visiting a prostitute:

'This only happens to be what I have been dreaming about night and day since I am thirteen. At long last, not a cored apple, not an empty milk bottle greased with vaseline, but a girl in a slip, with two tits and a cunt – and a moustache, but who am I to be picky?'

Be sparing, then, with humour, if you are writing an erotic novel; if you want to try your hand at a comic novel about sex, that is another matter. But in that case skill in the writing is much more important than an apprehension of what may turn readers on.

7
Erotic
poetry

Many poets have written highly erotic poetry; but this is not a book about how to do so – indeed, the whole idea of teaching someone to write poetry who does not feel the impulse to do so must be highly suspect. However, there is one good reason why you, who want to write erotic prose, should give some attention to reading erotic verse: reading, and trying to write, verse can actually improve your prose style (it's a tip I would give to any sort of writer). Writing verse in a strict metrical form (and I'm not talking about writing prose you then chop up into short lines) improves one's sense of rhythm and form, and sharpens the verbal sense.

Erotic poetry – like erotic prose – is as old as writing. The Greek Anthology is full of splendidly lecherous short poems, and certainly Catullus (c84-54BC) is well worth reading for his wit, ingenuity, irony – and polymorphous perversity! As far as good erotic poetry in English is concerned, rather than the bawdy of Norman monks and of Chaucer's *Canterbury Tales*, it perhaps starts with the period of that wonderful poem of Sir Thomas Wyatt (1503-1542), *The Forsaken Lover*, which begins 'They flee from me that sometime did me seek/ With naked foot stalking in my chamber. . .' And from then on, there are great riches from Spenser and Shakespeare, Marlowe and Campion, to Donne (whose amorous poems carry perhaps a stronger erotic charge than almost any others) and on through Rochester to Byron and Swinburne and more modern poets.

Anyone searching for the best verbal expression of what it is to love, physically and emotionally, cannot possibly neglect to read Donne – from the deeply spiritual to the wildly sensual:

'Licence my roving hands, and let them go
Before, behind, between, above, below.
O my America, my new found land,
My kingdom, safeliest when with one man manned. . .

'Full nakedness, all joys are due to thee.
As souls unbodied, bodies unclothed must be,
To taste whole joys. . .

'To teach thee, I am naked first, why then
What needst thou have more covering than a man?'

This is the most civilised kind of erotic writing, whether in verse or prose: witty, intelligent, full of verbal play which is as delightful as the physical pleasure about which the poet writes.

John Wilmot, Earl of Rochester (1647-80), is a writer of quite another sort, much of whose writing is scabrous and obscene – but who can also be thoughtfully and even tenderly erotic. His *A Ramble in St James's Park* yields to no-one in obscenity:

'Much wine had passed, with grave discourse
Of who fucks who and who does worse. . .
When I, who still take care to see
Drunkenness relieved by lechery,
Went out into St James's Park
To cool my head and fire my heart. . .'

He goes on to describe the various erotic activities in the Park (as profligate and varied in the seventeenth century as in our own):

'Full gorgéd at another time
With a vast meal of nasty slime
Which your devouring cunt had drawn
From porters' backs and footmen's brawn,
I was content to serve you up
My bollock-full for your grace cup. . .'

Not what you would call especially sensitive or witty. Yet the same man could write that wonderful poem *A song of a Young Lady to her Ancient Lover*, the final verse of which runs:

'Thy nobler part, which but to name
In our sex would be counted shame,
By age's frozen grasp possessed
From their ice shall be released
And soothed by my reviving hand
In former warmth and vigour stand.
All a lover's wish can reach
For thy joy my love shall teach
And for thy pleasure shall improve
All that art can add to love.
Yet still I love thee without art,
Ancient person of my heart.'

In our own time there have been a number of excellent erotic poets, both heterosexual and homosexual, both sensitive and downright orgiastic. Read the Greek poet C. P. Cavafy, Maureen Duffy, Thom Gunn, Kingsley Amis, Alex Comfort and above all Gavin Ewart. Most readers with an interest in poetry will know, probably by heart,

W. H. Auden's *Lay your sleeping head, my love*; fewer will have come across *The Platonic Blow*, a poem of his which was circulated for the most part from hand to hand, and only published under his name after his death. It is perhaps the best of all highly explicit gay poems:

'I scanned his tan, enjoyed the contrast of brown
Trunk against white shorts taut around small
Hips. With a dig and a wriggle he peeled them down.
I tore off my clothes. He faced me, smiling. I saw all.

'The gorgeous organ stood stiffly and straightly out
With a slight flare upwards. At each beat of his heart it threw
An odd little nod my way. From the slot of the spout
Exuded a drop of transparent viscous goo.

'The lair of hair was fair, the grove of a young man,
A tangle of curls and whorls, luxurious but couth.
Except for a spur of golden hairs that ran
To the neat navel the rest of the belly was smooth. . .'

John Betjeman's poems are full of sex, overtly expressed however only in his delightful couplet:

'I sometimes think I'd rather like
To be the saddle of a bike.'

Both poems are highly characteristic, and the internal rhymes, the sensitive rhythms lift the first from obscene doggerel into first-rate light verse – and remind us that whatever we are writing, it is worth trying to write well: the difference between *The Platonic Blow* and the lines on a lavatory wall is the difference between Conrad's *The Secret Agent* and a pot-boiling thriller .

Read, then, enjoy – and learn.

The limerick

A verse form particularly useful for those five-finger exercises which every writer, as every pianist, needs, is the limerick. This has been around in its modern form for over a century and a half: the first known collection came out in 1821 – *The History of Sixteen Wonderful Old Women*, written in the style that Edward Lear made popular, the last line ending with the same word as the first. The modern form is capable of being more ingenious and funnier; but alas it has fallen into desuetude, and very few good limericks now come to light. The number of published limericks which simply do not scan is shaming – and people who should know better encourage sloppiness. The weekend magazine section of one of the broadsheet daily papers recently held a limerick competition, and ignoring a fine and meticulously written verse by Gavin Ewart gave the prize to one which may or may not have been funnier, but which by no stretch of the imagination conformed to the rules of metre which make a limerick a limerick.

Again, it may seem strange to recommend someone interested in writing prose to study and even practise writing limericks, but to contrive a good one demands an inventive mind and a good sense of rhythm, as well as wit and humour; all of them invaluable to any writer. It is also instructive to study failed limericks, and limericks which have been damaged by publishers with tin ears. Here are two examples: one a very famous one, originally written by Professor A. H. Reginald Buller, F.R.S., Professor of Botany at the University of Manitoba, after reading about Einstein's Theory of Relativity. I have seen this reprinted as:

'There was a young lady named Bright
Whose speed was far faster than light;
   She went out one day
   In a relative way,
And returned the previous night.'

What Professor Buller originally wrote was:

'There was a young lady named Bright
Who could travel much faster than light.
   She set out one day
   In a relative way
And came back the previous night.'

To be boringly analytical, the second version avoids the unpleasant elision of 'Whose speed' and the unnecessary alliteration of 'far faster' (alliteration is a valuable trick, but must know its place); the first version ends with a line which simply does not scan (--/-/--/ instead of -/--/--/). Then there is the happy celebration of perversity at Cambridge, which originally went

'There was a young student of John's
Who attempted to bugger the swans.
   He was stopped by the porter
   Who said, 'Take my daughter -
The swans are reserved for the dons.'

This has appeared as

'There was a young student of John's
Who wanted to bugger the swans.
   But the loyal hall porter
   Said, 'Sir, take my daughter -
Them birds are reserved for the dons.'

I haven't much against the middle couplet, and 'Them birds' is quite fun; but 'attempted' is much funnier than 'wanted', and the metre with its unexpected little bump more interesting.

I mustn't carry on at length about the limerick as a sexual jolly (though there is a learned article to be written, no doubt, about why it so attracts smut, lavatory humour and sexual innuendo – and has from the beginning). But it does no harm to inject into a prose book the sense of sexual fun of the best of them – I just quote, finally, for simple pleasure:

> A handsome young plumber of Leigh
> Was plumbing a maid by the sea.
>   She cried: 'Cease your plumbing –
>   There's somebody coming!'
> 'I know,' said the plumber, 'it's me.'

No-one, I suggest, who could turn out a limerick like that could fail to write acceptable erotic prose!

8
Selling
your work

There is not a great deal more to be said about selling an erotic novel than about selling any other kind of book – except that it would be more than usually silly to submit it to the sort of publisher who simply does not publish erotica. The time may come when the Clarendon Press may be prepared to consider your *Virgin Tigresses*, but it is not yet.

However, the situation has certainly changed a great deal during the past few years. The new tolerance of pornographic fiction – or at least the large lack of opposition to it – together with a recession which has honed the eagerness of publishers to make money has to a large extent overcome their hesitation to publish books normally outside their range, and a number of highly respectable firms which a decade or so ago would have hesitated to be associated with any novel randier than, say, *Little Women*, now happily publish pornography – though of course not calling it that: Mills and Boon, for instance, for many years the publishers of almost excessively harmless romances, have in recent years allowed their writers to be a great deal franker about sex, and other publishers who put a toe in the water a few years ago by publishing 'serious' novels with some explicit sexual scenes now venture a great deal further. It is some years since John Updike's *Couples* introduced innocent readers to cunnilingus, and Philip Roth in America and Brian Aldiss in England wrote at length and in loving detail about masturbation – two topics that no conventional publisher would have issued before 1960.

One problem about publishers' still rather tentative approach to erotica is that it is not necessarily very helpful for a writer to look to those useful reference books the *Writers' and Artists' Yearbook* and *The Writer's Handbook* for help in deciding to whom to submit work. A far better idea (this is, as a matter of fact, true of any kind of fiction) is to go down to your nearest large bookshop and simply look along the shelves for a book similar to the one you have written or intend to write, and make a note of its publisher.

This is the way to discover markets for your shorter work, also.

There is a much smaller market for erotic short stories, and a diminutive one for verse. Erotic magazines depend chiefly on photographic material, with very brief captions of the 'Langorous Emily (42, 32, 48) loves flowers and spends her spare time studying the poems of Donne' variety. There are at the time of writing a very few British magazines which are interested in erotic fiction (*Desire*, published by Sky magazine, is perhaps the most prominent); there are more American magazines, but it is often difficult to find them in British stores, and a researcher friend in the U.S. is probably necessary.

There is of course some difficulty indeed in this country in that what you may need is not your nearest Smith's or Waterstone's but your nearest airport or motorway service station bookstall – for some of the large bookshops are still a little hesitant about stocking anything which might shock some of their customers. Here again, the situation is changing: both Smith's and Waterstone's now stock books they would not have touched a few years ago. Smith's for instance stock the Black Lace books of erotica for women, though they decline to stock very many erotic books for men (I can only suppose that their buyers have not actually read any Black Lace books, whose writers could give any male author a run for his money where explicit and often violent sex is concerned). The best bet for a really substantial over-view of what is available is to don your oldest mackintosh and make for Soho.

Unsolicited manuscripts

Having decided on a publishing house which might be interested in your idea, it is a mistake simply to post them 350 pages of manuscript. There is nothing to stop you doing so, of course; but the chances are that you are letting yourself in for a wait of at least six months before you get a reaction. The delay will *not* mean that your MSS will not be read. Contrary to popular belief, publishers *do* read unsolicited manuscripts: they are as eager to discover new talent as the new talent is to be discovered. But in the natural course of things, unsolicited MSS go to the bottom of the waiting list, below those commissioned or submitted by known writers, or by respected authors' agents. Apart from anything else, publishers are not short of good writers of erotic fiction: many of them issue at least a couple of such books a month, and most writers expect, once they have proved their worth, to be commissioned to provide one or two of these a year. Naturally, a publisher who already commissions a couple of dozen erotic novels a year tends to be very careful indeed before committing himself to more writers who will expect similar commissions.

It may well be a good idea in the first place to write a brief letter asking whether the publisher on whom you have your eye is actually looking for new writers. Because the erotic list is generally speaking only a relatively minor part of a publisher's entire output, it may be that he is (perhaps only for the time) closed to any new approaches.

By far the best idea, should the answer be a yes, is to send not the whole book (supposing that you have completed it) but a one-page summary of the plot and a chapter or two – not necessarily, though probably advisably, including the first. Any publisher should be able to judge the calibre of your writing from 4,000 – 5,000 words, though most prefer 10,000 or even 15,000. The work you send should of course be as representative of the tone of the whole book as you can make it: it should start with a bang (if not a bonk), and be as uninhibited and entertaining as you can make it. What a publisher is looking for is proof that you can write about sex with enthusiasm, originality, enjoyment and if possible a certain amount of wit (which does not mean that he wants a *funny* book, but that too dead-pan an approach can be self-defeating).

Sample text also proves to him that you can write competently and with a decent command of grammar, syntax and punctuation (yes, all these can of course be corrected by an editor, but no publisher is going to want to go to that expense of money and time). However bright your ideas, if you can't put them over in reasonable prose, no-one is going to be interested in them: there are successful books heavily rewritten by editors, but they are usually the products of people with a name which is sufficiently famous to sell the book whatever its merit or whoever has really written it.

At the risk of being too obvious, do make sure your MS is typed in double spacing on one side only of A4 paper, and that the pages are numbered but not bound. Leave decent margins; make sure your typewriter ribbon is still sufficiently inky, and remember that if there is anything publishers' readers hate more than a faint typewriter ribbon it is a dim dot matrix print-out. If you haven't a decent laser-quality printer, forget it, and send your disk to be printed by someone who has.

Start each chapter on a fresh page; the first line of each new chapter should be flush with the left-hand margin – indent the first lines of subsequent paragraphs. Beware of the three dot syndrome. . . It is infuriating if used too often. 'Single quotation marks' are now common, "doubles" only for quotes or remarks inside conversation. Don't put full-stops after titles such as Mr or Ms, Dr or Fr. The general rule about abbreviations is that full-stops come only when the abbreviation does not end with the final letter of the full word.

Presentation pays off

All this may seem tedious and unnecessary advice, but it is always worth paying attention to the presentation of your material, whatever the nature of your book; it is a form of politeness that always pays off – not that the most impeccably presented illiterate rubbish will sell, but a publisher will be more likely to read it with attention than a slovenly MS typed in single-spacing in illegible type.

Do enclose a stamped and addressed envelope with a letter, and *sufficient postage to return any MS you submit.* This may sound unimportant, but I assure you that it is. The simple question of how much postage to send with your MSS can be solved by taking it and the packaging to the post office and weighing them together before actually packing. Publishers don't usually much care for the idea of sending MS back to writers by registered post, or even recorded delivery; it simply makes things difficult for an often over-worked staff. But in any case you will of course have kept a duplicate, either on disc or in carboncopy or photocopy.

There is nothing to stop you, after submitting a synopsis and single chapter of a novel to a publisher, going on to write the whole of it on spec, if you wish. In writing, as in any other profession, practise is all, and no time spent on it is lost. The lessons you learn in writing your first erotic book will stand you in good stead if and when you go on to write your second, even should the first remain unpublished. In fact if you are a natural writer rather than someone who simply wants to 'be a writer', you will probably do this anyway.

As to length: you should aim at something over 80,000 words – certainly not under. Unless you produce a quite extra-ordinary MS, a publisher is unlikely to want anything too much longer than, say, 100,000, while anything under 80,000 will present him with costing problems. Good word-processing packages have word-counting facilities; you could aim to produce, say, fifteen chapters of more or less 5,500 words each – the format of most erotic books makes such a regular division a great deal easier than in books in which the plot is more complex than you are likely to want or need to make it.

Do you need an agent?

It is probably as difficult, these days, to get a good agent as to find a publisher; and the prospect of interesting an agent in you if you are aiming only or mainly to write erotica is even slimmer (though not perhaps by too much) than if you are a writer of general fiction. This is not because agents are mealy-mouthed about talking to publishers about erotica, but because there isn't going to be enough money in a series of erotic novels to make it worth their while to take you on. The average agent in the 1990s is not likely to be very interested in signing up a new writer who is not going to be able to make an income somewhere in the region of £25,000/£30,000 a year from writing – or unless the agent believes that the work is promising enough to suggest that a large income may be possible in a few years' time.

At present rates, unless you turn out to be exceptionally talented and find a publisher prepared to market your books enthusiastically, you would have to write half a dozen moderately successful erotic novels a year to get anywhere near the income necessary to interest an agent.

(Don't be too hard on the agent who turns you down: his income from your £30,000 a year will reasonably be £3,000; when you consider that he will probably have a West End office to maintain, with council tax, staff, telephones, postage, his is not an untenable attitude.)

The problems about not having an agent are not great and certainly not insoluble. Agents certainly know (or should know) what is going on in the publishing trade – who is looking for this kind of material or that, for instance – and will off the top of their heads have a better idea than you to whom to submit material. But by the simple process of looking along the bookshop shelves you can yourself come to a reasonably accurate conclusion about that. A more serious problem comes when your book has been accepted, and you receive a contract.

For goodness' sake do *not* be prompted by delight into signing the contract immediately and returning it by the next post. Read it carefully. You may find that some of it confuses you – and taking it to your solicitor is not likely to be a great deal of help, because it may confuse him, too, if he has no experience of publishing contracts. Fortunately the Society of Authors will happily check it for you, against their own experience and against the provisions of the Minimum Terms Contract which they have negotiated on behalf of their members with many publishers. They will of course hope if not expect that you will join the Society when your book has been published, and that will indeed be to your advantage if you intend to go on writing.

Pseudonyms

Most writers of erotica prefer to publish under a pen-name or pseudonym. While erotica is widely and freely published and extensively and enjoyably read, to be known as the author of erotic books is still for some reason not considered a matter about which writers on the whole want to boast. It is not easy to decide quite why: writing is not an easy job, and writing saleable books which do actually sell argues a certain amount of skill, in which one might be forgiven for taking some pride. Ask yourself, however, to how many even of your closest friends you would be happy to boast that you had just sold your fifteenth erotic novel? Some, yes; but many?

A pseudonym preserves your anonymity, if you want it protected. You should be careful not to choose a name similar to that of another author (the current edition of *Books in Print* will offer a list of those who currently have books in the shops. There are penalties for calling yourself, say, Barbara Cartland; but your publisher will be on the watch, too, for any slip-ups here).

Some authors who find it undesirable to be well-known for writing erotica but repugnant to hide as though ashamed, find a half-way house in leaving their names off the jacket and title-page, but printing it elsewhere (in the notice protecting their cultural rights, for instance). The choice is yours. It is true, of course, that a pseudonym will protect you from the writers of loony letters. For every letter from a handsome and desirable reader offering you his or her body in the course of research, there are likely to be ten from committed members of some League of Purity writing on lined paper in green ink to tell you off for promoting the enjoyment of sex. To which the proper answer is Henry Miller's, who asked for his comments by an Oslo court prosecuting *Sexus* for obscenity asserted that he was 'not to be indicted as a "pervert" or "degenerate", but simply as one who makes sex pleasurable and innocent!' His point was that for most protestors sex in fiction seems to be apparently alright if it is grim or uninviting; not if it is enjoyable.

Editors and editing

You will hear many authors complaining about the editing of their books, and indeed publishers' offices sometimes produce editors who, unable to originate books of their own, compose them vicariously by rewriting those of others. Happily, they are rarely ambitious to work on erotic MSS, and you are more likely to find that your editor is one of the many conscientious and hard-working ones who read your MS carefully and confine themselves to suggesting alterations where your grammar or the continuity of the story has gone awry. You will, or certainly should, have your MS returned to you with suggested alterations, before it goes to the printer. Check these scrupulously, and indeed take the opportunity of rereading your book through carefully while it is still in this state: making alterations in proof can be an expensive luxury. When you do get the book in proof form, confine yourself if you can to correcting typographical errors, and do no rewriting that is not absolutely necessary. If you do too much, your publisher may invoke the clause that will certainly be in your contract, and charge you for the extra sum the printer exacts from them for making those alterations.

There are, by the way, some anomalies regarding the marks which proof-readers make to indicate changes in MSS. It is probably best to rely on those set out in the *Writers' and Artists' Yearbook*; but whatever you do, do go by one or other of the published lists of such marks, otherwise you will give your publisher's editor more work, and/or confuse the printer.

Fame and fortune?

You may expect neither of these – barring accidents. It is conceivable that your book may be regarded as so unbelievably degenerate that it will be prosecuted for obscenity. Alternatively you may give one of your characters a name or nature which seems to suggest that it is based on a living person, and be sued for libel – in which case your name will become a household word, and after the prosecution has failed on the one count (for juries are these days almost unanimously unwilling to convict the authors and publishers of pornography, possibly because a number of them enjoy reading it) or succeeded on the other, your book will sell in hundreds of thousands as the result of the publicity.

It is much more likely, however, that at best it will sell steadily, and the most you can reasonably hope for is that your name – or pseudonym – will become well known to a number of readers who will look out for it on the spine of future books. You will probably not want publicity, and in any event will not get it. The possibility of your publisher organising a coast-to-coast book-signing tour is a slim one, though I guess the first well-publicised tour by an erotic author might have surprisingly encouraging results.

As to the amount of money you will make, your publisher may well not be prepared to offer you a first contract on the basis of a synopsis and sample chapter alone. He will want to see the finished MS first, so the most he is likely to do is say that he likes what you have done, and encourage you to complete the book. If he likes the finished article, he will then offer you a contract, and maybe an advance of £2,000 or thereabouts against royalties. What this means is that you will get a cheque for half that sum on signing the contract, and one for the other half on the day of publication. Your book will then have to sell sufficiently well to make that sum for the publishers before you get a further payment.

You will probably receive a royalty of 7½ percent of the published price on each copy sold. Since your book will almost certainly be published in paperback, its price will probably be in the region of £4.99 (call it £5, which is what the publishers would charge if they didn't have the idea that a round sum somehow puts people off). If you sell 10,000 copies in the first year, your total income from the book (at 7½ percent, or 37½p per copy) will be £3,750. If the publisher keeps your book in print it may well continue to sell fairly steadily; but you will scarcely make a fortune, even if you write two or three a year (which anyway may be more than your publisher wants). On the other hand, your success will of course be proportionate to the popularity of your book, and one or two of the Black Lace books have sold in the region of 30,000, which must mean something in the region of £11,500 for their authors. Successful magazines may pay about £150/£180 per thousand words for short stories, though the rate varies widely.

If you are moderately successful, you can argue with your publisher for a commission for following books, and suggest that your advance might rise to, say, £5,000. If he doesn't want to lose you, he will agree.

Sagas?

There is no reason, once you have established a period and characters, why you should not go on writing about them until your invention fails; many readers, if they like a character, enjoy following him or her through a series of adventures, and there is no reason why this precept should not work for erotic fiction as much as for thrillers or romances. On the other hand you may prefer the diversity of writing about various characters and various periods. But it is best to take your publisher's advice. One publisher received from a book club the advice that their readers did not like erotic novels set outside Britain, and would they kindly persuade their author to refrain from setting his books in the colonies?

What publishers want

Though you can best find out what publishers want by looking at the books they have already published, most firms do issue guidelines describing the kind of material they hope to receive from would-be writers, and Virgin have kindly allowed me to quote from theirs. First, their attitude to their Nexus list – 'erotic fiction for men'.

The writer is warned against pretension: 'our readers want a sexy story. They want to be able to understand what's going on, with a minimum of effort. They don't want to be distracted by extravagant vocabulary or complicated syntax.' Non-contemporary and foreign settings provide challenges which may defeat some authors, and it is suggested that you might do best to avoid them; on the other hand some very successful Nexus titles have been set in far-away places with strange-sounding names.

As to the sexual situations in the books: anything goes, Virgin say – though they do add, 'except as stated below.' Their advice on what is out of bounds concurs very much with what I say above (p.74 and see p.105), so I won't recapitulate. The paragraphs on this subject end with an admirable quotation from Graham Greene, commending a particular book as 'a rare thing, a pornographic book well written and without a trace of obscenity.' While the book about which he was writing was *The Story of O*, which is not a favourite of mine, Greene's sentiment is the right one. We are back to Oscar Wilde again: a well-written book really can deal with any subject.

Headline offer much the same advice as Virgin: 'the sex should be between consenting adults, i.e. over sixteen years of age, and should not contain any illegal activity'. The Managing Editor adds that 'toilet games are also out, if only because the editor can't stomach them'! This company has just begun to issue erotic books which are directed at a market both of men *and* women; the guide-lines are much the same as for single-sex erotica, and indeed there does not seem to be a great deal of difference between their earlier publications and the most recent ones – except that the tone of them does seem to be changing slightly.

This is of course inevitable. At present, the trend seems to be towards rather coarser material, and certainly away from period settings. This however seems to be a trend confined to this particular publisher and this particular line; elsewhere, Victoriana still abounds.

It has always been the rule with what might be called 'mass-produced' erotica that the important thing is the sex rather than the way in which it is presented, but the trend in the late 1990s seems to have been increasingly towards rough and increasingly crude language; Cleland, with his almost poetic language, would have a hard time today. Having said that, it is no more difficult, and no easier, to write erotic fiction than it ever was. For the erotic or pornographic writer it has perhaps always been true that he writes primarily for himself, and censorship has been the last thing to worry him – if only because for considerable periods of time it has been illegal for him to publish, so that the question didn't arise. The fact that these days anything, or almost anything, goes doesn't affect the situation. The only thing that does so is fashion, which operates here as everywhere else – and operates chiefly in the minds of publishers, for what the public wants, in this area of writing, is a constant; trends in presentation are the result of competition between publishers, their desire for 'something new'. But in this field, more than in any other, there is nothing new under the sun, and a writer who can convey basic sexuality vividly, with enthusiasm, vigour and a certain among of humour, is as likely to be successful as he ever was.

Afterward

Sex has almost always been a dangerous game. Before the invention of the condom there was always the danger of pregnancy; and the danger too of infection with some highly unpleasant, and often fatal, sexually transmitted disease. With the arrival of penicillin, we thought we were safe, and for a brief decade or so the game was afoot. Then came AIDS.

On the opening page of Jackie Collins' *American Star* (1992) the publishers, Heinemann, printed the following paragraph, it seems at Ms Collins' request:

> 'While *American Star* contains descriptions of unprotected sex appropriate to the period in which the story is set, both the author and the publisher want to emphasise the importance of practising safe sex and the use of condoms. Play it safe! Do not play with your life.'

Ideally, perhaps such a note should appear in every erotic novel (the Black Lace and Nexus imprints do include a briefer note). But after all, it is unlikely that the readers of erotic fiction need to be reminded that they are vicariously indulging their own fantasies; that the books have nothing whatsoever to do with real life; and that if condoms do not appear in every sex scene (they do appear in most contemporary pornographic movies and videos) that does not mean that anyone considers them unnecessary. Moreover, there is strong evidence to suggest that most readers of erotic fiction are aged between 25 and 40, and relatively well educated (despite the research supplied by Virgin Publishers). It should be unnecessary to read them warnings. Ironically, one of the critical reactions to Maureen Freely's *Under the Vulcania* was that there were too many condoms in it: 'condoms are not romantic.'

Fantasy or no fantasy, it seems sensible for writers to avoid descriptions of the obviously unsafe aspects of sexuality: the mixing of body fluids, for instance. Flagellation and anal sex are not going to disappear from erotic books (they are far too popular with readers to do that) but detailed descriptions of ejaculation or the mixing of blood should probably be avoided – as indeed should descriptions of ejaculation in the mouth during oral sex (though this is only dangerous in 'real life' if there are lesions through which the HIV virus can be transmitted).

There are other areas which are best avoided for one reason or another. There have been no cases, as far as I know, in which a writer or publisher has been prosecuted for describing under-age sex, but (even if your publisher does not object, and he is very likely to do so) it is clearly as offensive to write in detail about paedophilia as it is to depict it in photographic magazines. Whatever one's view about the age of consent, society decides what proscriptions to put on sex between consenting people, and the law should be observed.

Virgin's editors affirm that while they have no objection to sado-masochism or bondage, either in the Black Lace or Nexus books, they 'won't publish a novel which encourages or condones hatred of women; or which suggests that all women should be, or enjoy being, subjugated to men; or which includes bloodshed or wounding or emotional anguish as a result of sexual activities.' One would hope that a writer's good sense would have brought him to that conclusion already. One hesitates to talk of 'good taste': the phrase sits uneasily in a discussion of sex, whether on the page or in the bed. Sex is such a primitive force that it demands strong language. But on paper as in our personal behaviour we must set our own bounds: contrary to what Aleister Crowley believed, 'Do what you will' is *not* the whole of the law, and this is true even of fantasy.

Bibliography

Here is a relatively brief list of books which include, to a greater or lesser degree, distinguished examples of erotic writing. They are all worth reading and from each there are lessons to be learned. First, fiction:

Fredrica Alleyn: *Cassandra's Conflict* (1993)
Anon: *Eros in the Country* (1988)
Guillaume Apollinaire: *The Amorous Adventures of Prince Mony Vibesco* (1907)
Georges Bataille: *The Story of the Eye* (1928)
Aubrey Beardsley: *The Story of Venus and Tannhauser* (1907)
Jean de Berg: *The Image* (1956)
William Burroughs: *The Naked Lunch* (1959)
Kate Chopin: *The Awakening* (1899)
Colette: *Chéri* (1907)
Shirley Conran: *Lace* (1982)
Portia da Costa : *Gemini Heat* (1994)
Marguerite Duras: *The Lover* (1984)
Jean Genet: *Our Lady of the Flowers* (1943)
Alan Hollinghurst: *The Swimming Pool Library* (1988)
Frank Harris: *My Life and Loves* (1926)
Violette Leduc: La Bâtarde (1964)
Li You: *The Before Midnight Scholar* (tr. Richard Martin, 1959)
Henry Miller: *Tropic of Cancer* (1934)
Yukio Mishima: *Thirst for Love* (1950)
Anaïs Nin: *Delta of Venus* (1969); *Little Birds* (1979)
Robert Nye: *Falstaff* (1976)
Derek Parker (ed.) *An Anthology of Erotic Poetry* (1980); *An Anthology of Erotic Prose* (1981)
Pauline Réage: *The Story of O* (1954)

'Hughes Rebell' (Georges Grassall): *The Memoirs of Dolly Morton* (1899)
Philip Roth: *Portnoy's Complaint* (1969)
Terry Southern: *Blue Movie* (1973)
Terry Southern and Mason Hoffenburg: *Candy* (1968)
Gore Vidal: *Myra Breckinridge* (1968)
Anne-Marie Villefranche: *Plaisir d'Amour* (1982)
'Walter': *My Secret Life* (c.1890)
Emile Zola: *Nana* (1880)

Then non-fiction – books which not only give information, but provide ideas and stimulate the imagination:

John Atkins: *Sex in Literature* (three volumes, 1970-78)
Alex Comfort: *The Joy of Sex* (1971)
Nancy Friday: *Men in Love* (1988); *Women on Top* (1991)
Patrick J. Kearney: *A History of Erotic Literature* (1982)
Alfred C. Kinsey (ed., with others): *Sexual Behaviour in the Human Male; Sexual Behaviour in the Human Female* (1953)
Jane Mills (ed.): *Bloomsbury Guide to Erotic Literature* (1993)
G. L. Simons (ed.): *The Illustrated Book of Sexual Records* (1974)
Eric J. Trimmer (ed.): *The Visual Dictionary of Sex* (1978)
Irving Wallace (ed., with others): *The Intimate Sex Lives of Famous People* (1981)
C. Willett and Phyllis Cunnington: *The History of Underclothes* (1992)
The Kama Sutra of Vatsyayana, *The Ananga-Ranga of Kalyana Malla, The Perfumed Garden of Sheikh Nefzawi* (all translated by Sir Richard Burton)

The best book about author/publisher dealings – from submitting a MS to seeing your book on sale, is
An Author's Guide to Publishing, by Michael Legat (1991)

Index

Learning Resources
Centre